Frank Lloyd Wright in Michigan

Frank Lloyd Wright in Michigan

A. Dale Northup

1991

"A Habitat Book"

REFERENCE PUBLICATIONS, INC.
Algonac, Michigan

Published in 1991

NO 4 IN THE SERIES ''MICHIGAN MONOGRAPHS''

''A Habitat Book''

Library of Congress Catalogihg in Publication Data

Northup, A. Dale, 1941-
Frank Lloyd Wright in Michigan/ A. Dale Northup.— [2nd rev. ed.]
p. cm.—(Michigan monographs; no. 4)
''A Habitat book.''
Includes bibliographical references and index.
1. Wright, Frank Lloyd, 1867-1959—Criticism and interpretation.
2. Usonian houses—Michigan. 3. Cottages—Michigan. 4. Prairie school (Architecture)—Michigan.
I. Title. II. Series.
NA737.W7N6 1991b
728'.373'092—dc20 91-43067
CIP

ISBN No. 0-917256-51-4
LC No. —91-43067

REFERENCE PUBLICATIONS, INC.
218 ST. CLAIR RIVER DRIVE
BOX 344, ALGONAC
MICHIGAN 48001

Dedication

To Helen Graves Northup, Mother and educator
and to the memory of Wayne Andrews.

''By wisdom
a house is built,
and by understanding
it is established...''

Proverbs 24:3, RSV

Contents

Acknowledgments 5

Preface 6

Foreword *by Grant Carpenter Manson* 8

1. The Prairie House 11

2. The Usonian House 31

3. Usonian Expansion 43

4. Efflorescence 73

Houses designed By Frank Lloyd Wright in Michigan 97

Appendix. 98

Index 102

Acknowledgments

My initial research efforts began with James Babcock, former Director of the Burton Historical Collection at the Detroit Main Library, who helped lay the groundwork. Bruce Brooks Pfeiffer, Director of the Frank Lloyd Wright Archives, has been a continuous source of information and inspiration particularly as regards to his own research and publications. Lynn Merrill-Francis, formerly with the Michigan Society of Architects, was helpful in compiling the listing of talks Frank Lloyd Wright gave in Michigan. I am also indebted to the many talented individuals who contributed to the visual material: Penelope Gwyn Peck; Bob Vieracker; and Dale Patrick Wolicki. Herbert Conlan assisted with the proofing of the text as well as lending moral support. Mary Woolever, Architecture Archivist with the Ryerson & Burnham Libraries, was helpful in clarifying some of the Chicago clients in Michigan. And, most of all, special thanks go to the clients of Frank Lloyd Wright in Michigan whose vision and enthusiastic character were instrumental in writing the book.

The Red Square (see cover) is a registered trademark belonging to the Frank Lloyd Wright Foundation; permission was granted for its use in this publication.

Preface

Visionary architects, who disturb established patterns, often stand firm with their ideas against an authoritarian bureaucracy who say ''no'' to architectural digression. Such was the case with Frank Lloyd Wright. He responded by saying, ''The codes are adamant,'' condemning the laws that were made contrary to the interests of the human being. Wright spent his entire life creating an architecture that would harmonize the human psyche with nature. Such a symbiotic relationship was paramount in Wright's philosophy of organic architecture. Also important was a design methodology serving the individual need for shelter while reflecting a democratic ideal. Consequently, Wright created an open plan based on such ideas as ''continuity'' and ''plasticity'' he espoused in his book *The Natural House*. As Jean Jacques Rousseau said, ''Man is born free and is everywhere in chains.'' Wright was intent on breaking those chains.

To what extent did the architecture of Frank Lloyd Wright satisfy the individual needs of his clients? In the last years of his life, Wright wrote, ''The true center (the only centralization allowable) in Usonian democracy is the individual in his Usonian home. In that we have the nuclear building we will learn to build.'' He believed this idea could be realized with an intelligent, understanding client.

The design principles of the Prairie House and the Usonian House will be discussed with special reference to the character of the client who chose to live in a house designed by Wright. What kind of individuals were they and what drew them to the architect? Many of Wright's clients were initially attracted to his architecture by his writings and photographic examples of his work. The average home owner is often romantically obsessed with historical associations in domestic architecture that visually convey a conventional life style. The owner of a Wright house is an individual more content with a design that provides ''a new sense of freedom.'' Consequently, they opened themselves to broader perspectives and a new way of living. In many ways, they too were visionaries helping to formulate a new architecture in the twentieth century—the architecture of Frank Lloyd Wright.

Frank Lloyd Wright designed over 1,000 structures of which 72 were houses in Michigan with 32 actually built. This number rates Michigan third, after Wright's home state of Wisconsin, and Illinois where he first practiced architecture in his early years. The Michigan houses Wright designed reflect his imaginative genius and the unique individuals who built them. With such an architect-client relationship, there was a perfect union that led to a ''natural performance'' in architecture.

A. DALE NORTHUP

Foreword

When intolerable heat-waves that grip the Ohio valley are briefly broken by ''cool spells'' and it is momentarily possible to draw breath again, the murmur arises on all sides: ''Ah-h, Michigan weather.'' Around the turn of the century, before the dawn of artificially-controlled temperature, overheated minds from Cincinnati to Louisville entertained visions of the two-tiered state to the north with its three-thousand-mile shore line on four of the Great Lakes, its deep forests (what had been left of them by the lumber barons) of pine, balsam and hemlock, its trout streams and placid inland lakes. It was a beckoning summer paradise, and it was a mere overnight journey by train.

The same scenario played out in Chicago's hinterland, the cornbelt, where escape to Michigan was even more alluring—an overnight trip by water eastward across the Lake on the ever-popular *Manitou* to such centers of summer paradise as Charlevoix, Harbor Springs, and Mackinac. If your own cottage awaited you upon arrival, you had it made.

Thus, by 1900, Michigan had become fixed in the minds of Midwesterners as a summertime refuge despite the fact that the state had also become industrialized. But its industries were confined to a narrow zone stretching from east to west across the bottom third of the lower peninsula. The summer influx could, and did, bypass it and ignore its existence. Above it to the north and northwest, in a climate perpetually cooled by breezes off the Lakes, was a country where life could still be led on a picturesque primitive level, where the oil lamp, woodsmoke in the air, the plash of the paddle, the cry of the loon symbolized escape. Inconveniences such as the outdoor privy were even welcomed as part of the picture.

To think that such a tolerance was easy because virtually nothing was then known of what have come to be life's indispensables—safe storage of foods by artificial refrigeration, control of temperature and humidity, indoor facilities with running water, telecommunications, rapid transportation by highway, etc., etc.—makes it hard to accept that we are speaking of a period of time in this, our 20th century. (That all these means of making our lives perpetually easy and comfortable was to entail the use of energy on so lavish a scale as to endanger our planet did not become clear until the closing years of the century, and by now we are hooked.)

Frank Lloyd Wright was associated with the business of the Michigan *villegiatura* from its inception, and from the earliest days of his professional career. People who came to the Studio in Oak Park to place a commission for a house frequently ordered its companion-piece, the Michigan cottage, at the same time. What was at the forefront of Wright's creative mind at this juncture was the exfoliation of the Prairie House, his first and perhaps his greatest architectural invention, the characteristics of which—stressed horizontality, low-pitched roof, low center of mass, open plan, ribbon fenestration—were as at home in the Michigan woods as on the Illinois prairie. So he turned out both commissions in its style; a big Prairie House and a little one, a year-round dwelling and a seasonal one.

This first phase of Wright's presence on the Michigan scene, roughly 1895-1915, was followed by a long blank during which he was not there at all. Actually, his practice, not only in the north woods, but on all fronts, nearly ground to a halt during the middle third of his life when personal irregularities and tragedies overwhelmed him. When, at last, by 1935, he had got his career back together again and was ready to re-establish himself as an architect of worldwide renown, the situation in Michigan, as elsewhere in the West, had changed out of mind. A major war had intervened, and Michigan industry had geared itself up to the job of supplying *materiel*, and had at the same time captured to itself the manufacture of that dramatic new means of transportation, the automobile, on which it was to hold a near-monopoly for decades to come. This new device, rapturously welcomed, penetrated all parts of the globe; no place was truly remote. So did the availability of electric power, the impact of which was total. To turn our attention again to Michigan, that part of the state north of 41′ 42′′ latitude was no longer escape country. Millions of Americans now worked and lived their entire lives there, only peripherally aware of the blessings of its climate. And the idea that once its main lines of entry were the vacation train and the vacation steamer seemed as quaint as the horse-and-buggy.

This is how it came about that Wright's activities in Michigan, both temporally and demographically, fall into two separate categories. What he built there up to 1915 was the seasonal dwelling—the summer cottage—and it was carried out in the Prairie House manner. What he built there after the long hiatus was year-round residences for permanent, regionally-employed inhabitants, and it was executed in the manner of the Usonian House, the replacement of the Prairie House, which circumstances had rendered obsolescent. Now let the author of this book present and analyze the unique nature of Wright's work in Michigan, in which he has specialized and in which he offers fascinating insights, as a result of his long research, and some hitherto little known examples of Wright's work in the two-tiered state.

Grant Carpenter Manson

1. The Prairie House

The proximity of Michigan to Illinois and Chicago was a natural consequence for an architectural diffusion of Frank Lloyd Wright's Prairie House to Michigan in the late nineteenth and early twentieth centuries. Many Chicagoans vacationed on the eastern, sandy shores, or in the lush woods, along Lake Michigan, to take a break from the intense summer heat of their native city. Some of these individuals were familiar with Wright's work in Chicago, so they commissioned Wright to design modest summer retreats for them in Michigan. One of these clients was Chicago businessman Arthur Heurtley. The project involved remodelling a cottage he owned at Les Cheneaux, an archipelago of islands in the northern waters of Lake Huron (Fig.1). It was the first Michigan dwelling designed, in part, by Wright in 1898. As planned, a new facade extension was wrapped around a pre-existing structure and considerably changed the exterior appearance while adding more room. The horizontal board and batten siding, with a canted base, bears a marked resemblance to the River Forest Golf Club (Fig. 2) which Wright designed the same year. The roofline flares out from the gabled ends of the Heurtley cottage to become the roof of the porch. This architectural detail is similar to the Harry C. Goodrich house in Oak Park (Fig. 3), designed by Wright in 1896. In a letter, dated July 19, 1908, to an artist-friend whom he patronized, Heurtley expressed his satisfaction with Wright:

> ... ready to go away for my holidays and nice coming here [Les Cheneaux]; where I have had a cottage for over ten years (also my friend Wright's work)...
>
> I wish you could know my friend Frank Lloyd Wright. I think you would like him: a man of fine education, a musician and artist ... a man of high ideals and aspirations...[1]

Four years later, in 1902, Wright returned to the Michigan woods at Whitehall, a former lumbering community turned resort. There he designed two cottages for brothers George and Walter Gerts who were Chicago businessmen. The dwelling for George is a ''double cottage'' (Fig. 4) both halves of which are a mirror reflection of the other with fireplaces back to back. The duality provided separate quarters for the owner and his guests. Each side had one bedroom with the large living room conceived by Wright as one open living space. Corner windows break down the confining features of the walls while also serving to integrate the interior with its surroundings. The cottage is entered by crossing over a bridge which fords a stream below. This structural element suggests Wright's sensitivity toward site orientation and portends his ''Fallingwater'' in Mill Run, Pennsylvania (1936). Walter Gerts' cottage (Fig. 5) is a single dwelling anchored to the site with a central chimney mass. It has a more spacious interior containing two bedrooms. The ribbon fenestration opens the interior to the outside and double sets of doors lead out to porches on either end of the dwelling. The two Gerts cottages have horizontal board and batten siding under shallow hip roofs which make them a ''Prairie House reduced to an incident in the Michigan forests.''[2]

The same year as the Whitehall projects, Wright designed another summer dwelling in Charlevoix, Michigan for a valuable Chicago client—Edward C. Waller—who was a major real estate developer in Chicago. He was an investor in the Home Insurance Building (1885) and the Tacoma Building (1886), both forerunners of the modern skyscraper. Also a leader in the growth and development of River Forest, where he lived, Waller lived across the street from the William H. Winslow house designed by Wright in 1893. Conservative as his personal living tastes were, Waller admired the Winslow house because he had seen something new and different. Subsequently, he commissioned Wright to design a new house for him in 1898. It was unexecuted because Waller might have felt conspicuous among his neighbors. Or, as another client admonished Wright about the design of his house, ''I don't want to go down backstreets to my morning train to avoid being laughed at...''[3]

In 1902, Waller commissioned Wright to design his summer residence at Charlevoix (Fig. 6) on less conspicuous ground. The house was an impressive structure for a seasonal dwelling which displayed many of the Prairie House features: cruciform in plan; wings centrifugally extending into the landscape; and bands of windows located under the large overhanging eaves of a shallow hip roof. The house was planned to be built on the crest of a slope with a retaining wall supporting an open ter-

Fig. 1. Arthur Heurtley cottage, Les Cheneaux, Michigan, 1898.

Fig. 2. River Forest Golf Club, River Forest, Illinois, 1898.

Fig. 3. Harry Goodrich house, Oak Park, Illinois, 1896.

race commanding a view of Lake Charlevoix beyond. This was scheme number one. A second dwelling (Fig. 7) was designed by Wright the following year. The latter was essentially the same plan but more modest in size. The scaling down of the second dwelling seems to suggest an exercise in cost containment for a summer residence that might have proven to be too expensive. Neither house was built.

In 1908, Wright designed two more houses in Michigan: the Meyer May house in Grand Rapids and the William Burke house in Three Rivers. These houses are relatively unsung works which have been upstaged by two oft-recognized dwellings designed by Wright the same year: the Frederick Robie house in Chicago and the Avery Coonley house in Riverside, Illinois. Meyer May commissioned Wright to design his residence on the corner of Madison and Logan Streets in southeast Grand Rapids. When May, a retail clothier, journeyed to Chicago to do his merchandise buying, he could have heard about Wright through casual conversation with some of his business associates. He also kept abreast with the latest in fashion apparel by reading local periodicals and might have seen one of the many current articles featuring Wright's work. Either one of these encounters could have served as a catalyst for the new house he was planning to build; subsequently, he commissioned Wright as the architect.

There is a marked similarity between the May house (Fig. 8) and the Robie house (Fig. 9): both are two-story brick structures located on corner city lots; they have widely overhanging hip roofs; the living room windows are framed with massive brick piers on the first floor. Coincidentally, one must pursue a circuitous route in order to find the front entrance to both dwellings. Unlike the Robie house, the May house has an extending wing, which is perpendicular to the main part of the house, accommodated by a wider lot. This allows it to interact more with the landscape in a typical Prairie House fashion.

The May house has many unique features of its own. The copper-clad grillwork, over the living room windows (Fig. 10), is an abstract interplay of rectilinear elements which extend upward with vertical extensions in front of the second story windows. This patterned motif evokes an association with the geometry of the Amerindic cultures which Wright admired

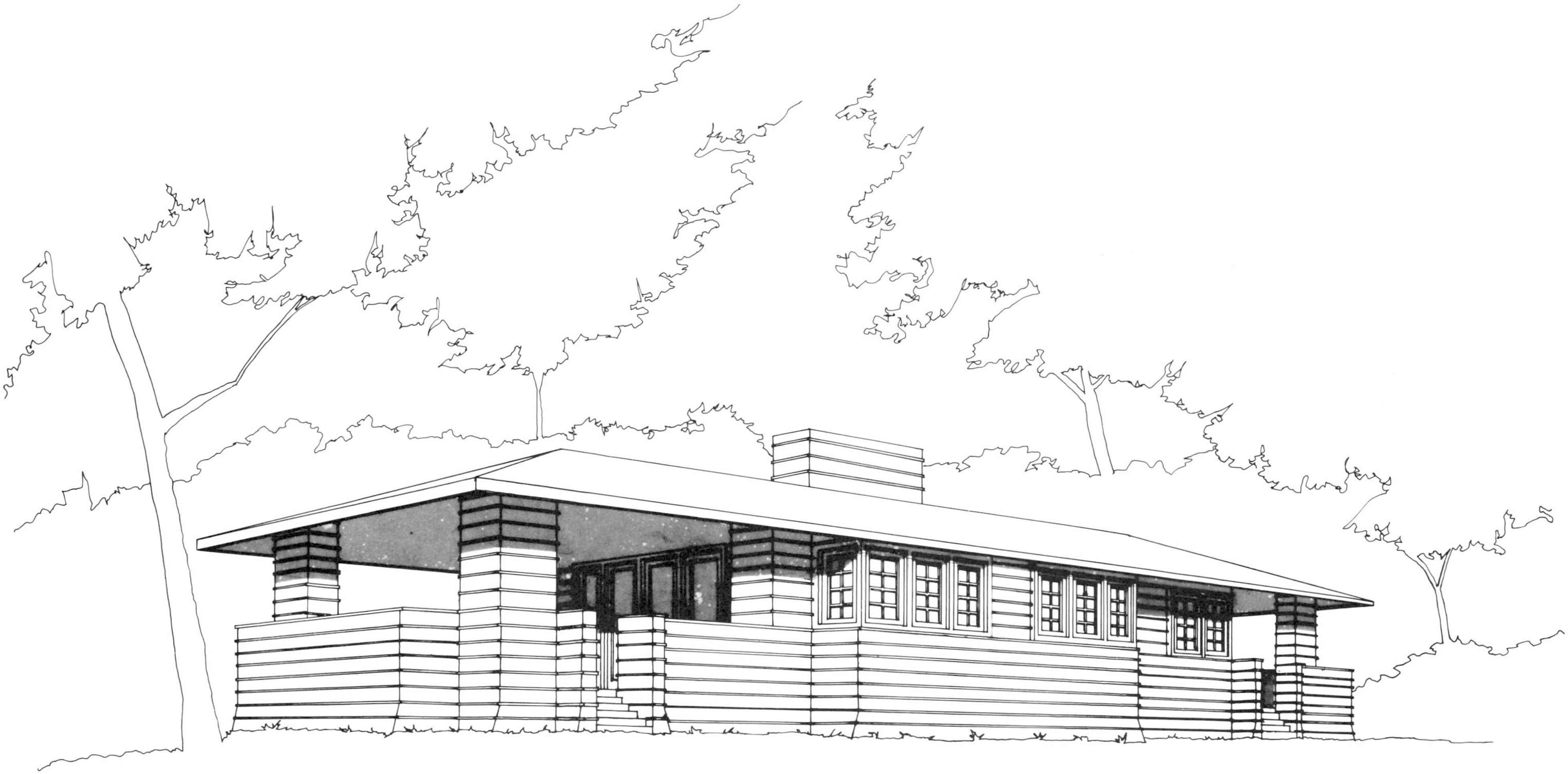

Rendering by Dale Patrick Wolicki

Fig. 4. George Gerts cottage, Whitehall, Michigan, 1902.

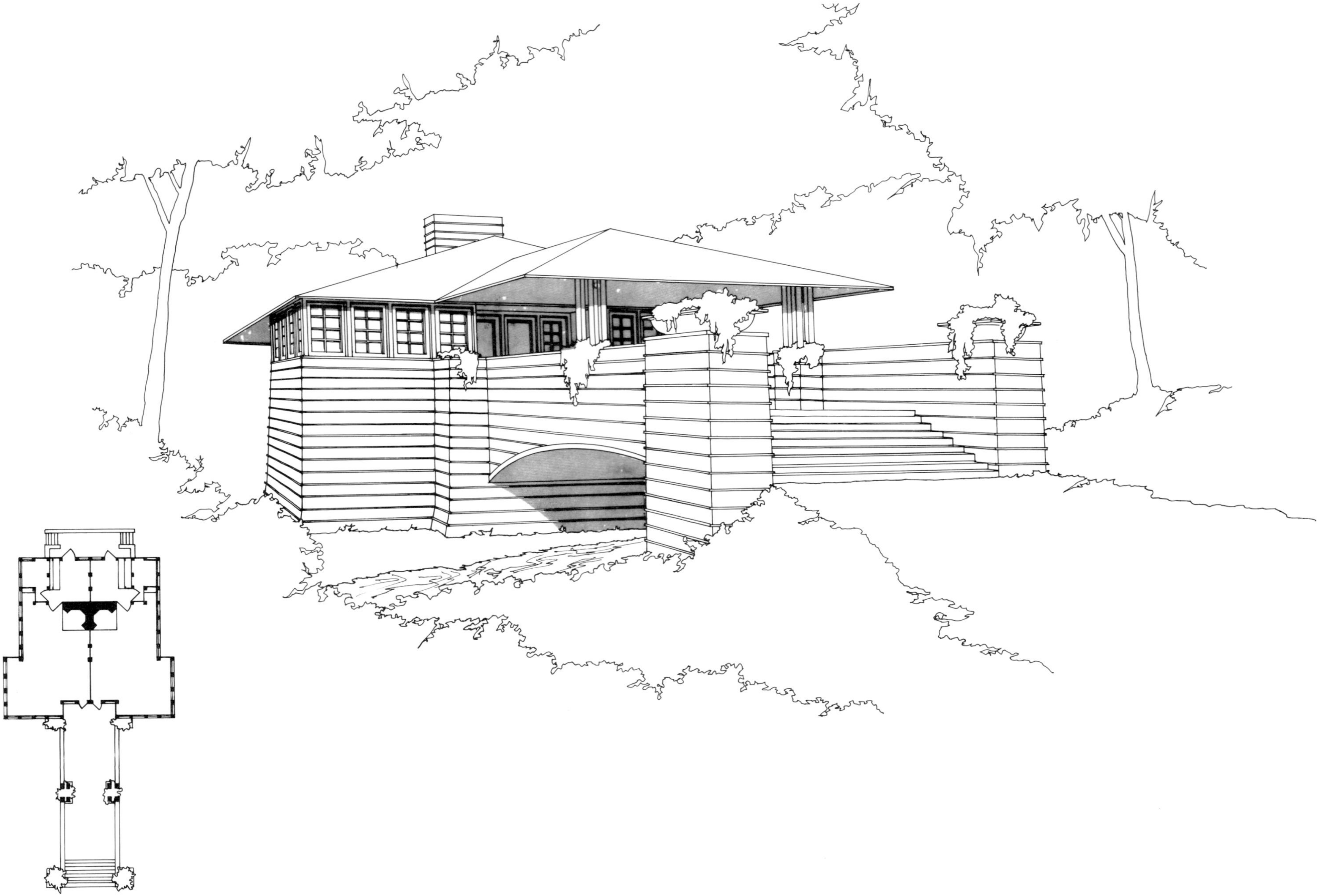

Rendering by Dale Patrick Wolicki

Fig. 5. Walter Gerts cottage, Whitehall, Michigan, 1902.

and referred to as ''great American abstractions.'' It is also a prognostication of Wright's Chicago Midway Gardens of 1913 (Fig. 11) with its amazing display of abstract ornament.

Once the hidden entrance is found to the May house, the entry hall inside is shallow and defined, opposite the front door, by a grille made of vertical oak slats around which are a series of rooms one flowing into the other. This was Wright's way of creating one open living space that he advocated in domestic architecture. The interior is visually expanded with large areas of windows that open to the exterior. Like so many of Wright's Prairie Houses, it was a space to be lived within and without at the same time.

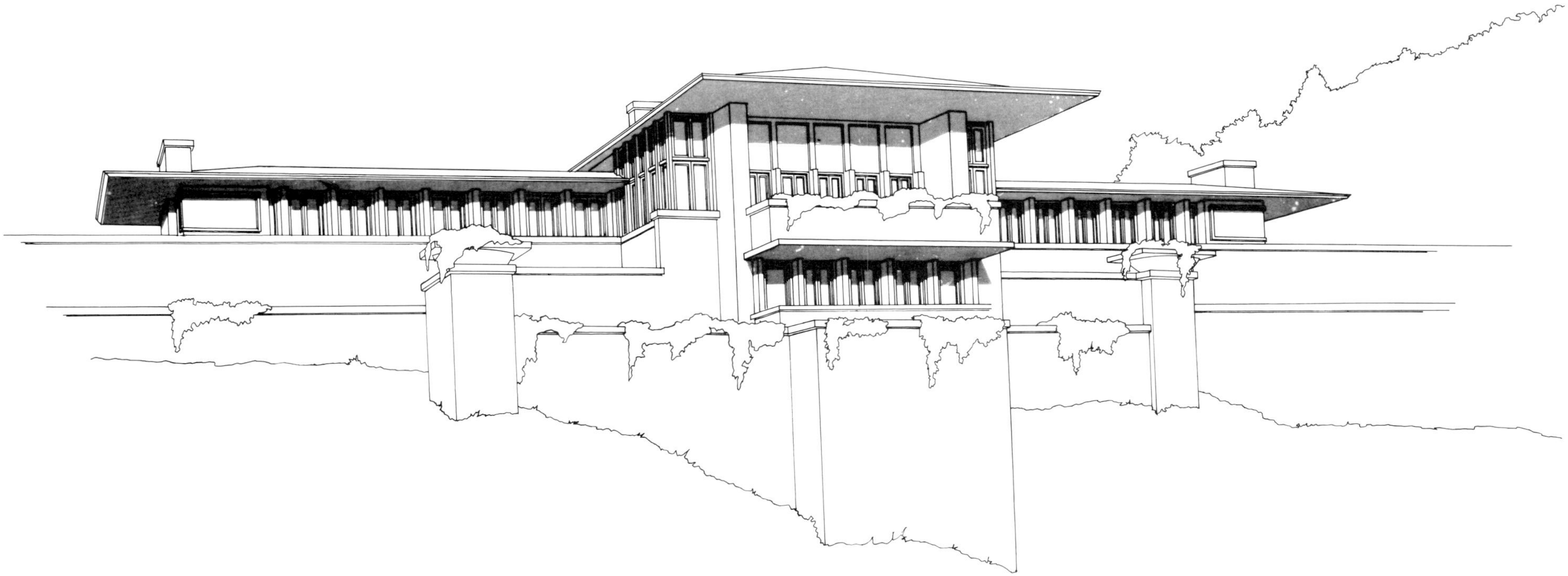

Rendering by Dale Patrick Wolicki

Fig. 6. Edward C. Waller summer residence, scheme #1, Charlevoix, Michigan, 1902.

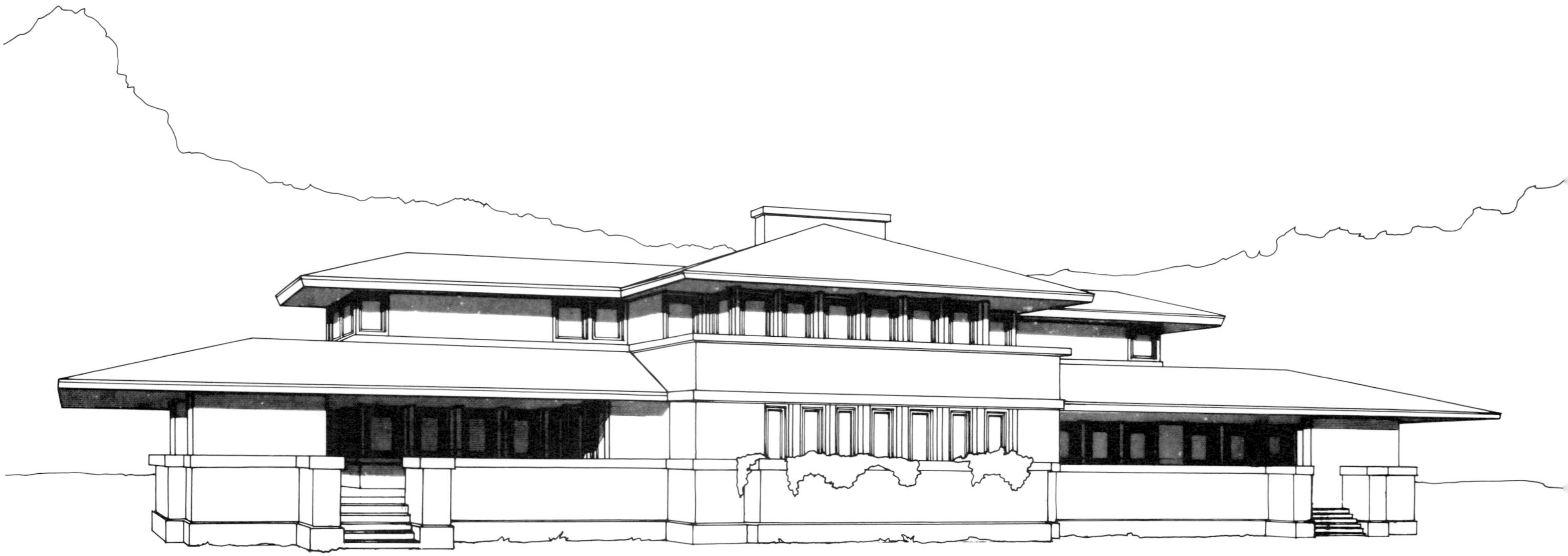

Rendering by Dale Patrick Wolicki

Fig. 7. Waller summer residence, scheme #2.

Hedrich-Blessing

Fig. 8. Meyer May house, Grand Rapids, Michigan, 1908.

Domino's Center of Architecture & Design

Fig. 9. Frederick Robie house, Chicago, Illinois, 1908.

Hedrich-Blessing

Fig. 10. Close-up view of Meyer May house, Grand Rapids, Michigan, 1908.

The William Burke house on North Main Street in Three Rivers was designed and built in 1908 and, unfortunately, torn down in 1965 (Fig. 12). Burke migrated to Three Rivers from Chicago to work as a publicity man for the R.M. Kellogg Company. While in Chicago, he was the publisher of *The Farmer's Voice* and, through his journalistic connections, he could have discovered the work of Frank Lloyd Wright. The Burke house was designed by Marion Mahony, the first woman registered to practice architecture in Illinois. She worked with Wright in his Oak Park Studio for thirteen years. Wright undoubtedly assigned this ''lesser'' project in Three Rivers to Mahony so he could concentrate on the major projects of that year, as well as supervising projects from the year before. It was a complete reworking of Wright's pattern house featured in the February, 1901 issue of *The Ladies Home Journal* (Fig. 13) titled ''A Home in a Prairie Town,'' which later contributed to the generic term Prairie House. This pattern house satisfied Burke's desire to build a house within a reasonably priced budget of six thousand dollars.

Mahony took liberties with the Burke house to make this essentially ''her'' design. She rearranged the floorplan placing the central living area of the house so that it would be perpendicular to the street. The projecting library wing, as outlined in the original design, was placed between the living room and the veranda of the Burke house. Less expensive board and batten siding was used on the exterior. The fenestration on the second floor was varied with bands of windows complemented by rectangular, windowed bays on the north and south sides of the house. This window treatment is also incorporated on the second story front of the May house. The similarity suggests that Mahony borrowed the motif since she worked on so many of the house elevation drawings for Wright that year.

Rectangular columns on the porch extended across the entire front of the house. They had a modular disposition which defined the living spaces behind them. Stucco was added later to serve as insulation against the harsh Michigan winters. The plan of the Burke house is similar to the inexpensive cubical-type houses Wright inaugurated in 1905 while retaining the long, roofed veranda characteristic of the more costly Robie house of the same year. Although awkwardly conceived, the Burke house can

Domino's Center of Architecture & Design

Fig. 11. Midway Gardens, Chicago, Illinois, 1913: demolished in 1929.

be viewed as one of the few realizations of Wright's pattern house published in *The Ladies Home Journal*. It does, however, re-affirm questions concerning the Wright-Mahony association. Despite Mahony's contribution to the work done in the Oak Park studio, "Wright accused her of stealing clients and architectural projects ..."[4] "... At what point their artistic personalities overlap or merge is a question that can never be answered with positive assurance."[5] The initial design conception of the Three Rivers house belongs to Wright. Its conversion can be attributed to Mahony. It may never be determined to what extent either was involved.

In 1909 Wright's architectural career plummeted when he embarked for Europe with a client's wife—Mamah Borthwick Cheney. (See Appendix B.) He explained the departure in his autobiography:

> ... This absorbing, consuming phase of my experience as an architect ended about 1909. I had almost reached my fortieth year. Weary, I was losing grip on my work and even my interest in it ... I could see no way out because I did not know what I wanted. I wanted to go away ...[6]

That year, however, could have been the apogee of Wright's career had he become involved with America's first billionaire, Henry Ford. Wright was contacted by Ford about a possible design for his new residence to be built on family land in Dearborn later to be called Fairlane. John van Bergen, who was with Wright the last year of his Oak Park Studio, recalled a meeting with Ford and "... Wright's inability to maintain his customary, self-confident manner."[7] Much speculation is given over to the interface involving the commission: "... Henry's non-conformist instincts led him to Wright;"[8] "Edsel suggested that he hire Frank Lloyd Wright as his architect but Henry was horrified by Wright's contemporary design."[9] These are certainly two conflicting views of which the former lends some credibility but the latter does not. Edsel would have been 16 years of age at the time and such an influence, which he did not exercise later in life on his father, raises serious questions. The logical intermediary was C. Harold Wills, Ford's business partner and confidant. Wills had artistic flair and mechanical ingenuity. "... He had a passion for mechanical design; often after dinner, according to his son [C. Harold Wills Jr.], he

Fig. 12. William Burke house, Three Rivers, Michigan, 1908.

Frank Lloyd Wright Archives

Fig. 13. *The Ladies Home Journal* pattern house, 1901.

would sit at the table designing plans and setting himself problems..."[10] These are attributes often associated with Wright's clients. Knowing that Ford was going to build, Wills was perhaps the inducer, sharing his enthusiasm and awareness of Wright's work with Ford in casual conversation. This dialogue could have served as the catalyst for the Ford-Wright encounter.

There are, however, no written documents that substantiate a contract between Ford and Wright. The meeting will remain as oral history unrecorded. Just as Henry Ford expanded America's industrial base, so too would Wright have further impacted American domestic architecture had the commission been realized. Wright closed down his Oak Park Studio turning the keys over to Hermann von Holst whom Ford would later commission for Fairlane as a consequence of his initial encounter with Wright. Wills had also enlisted von Holst to design his residence in Detroit prior to Ford which lends further credence to an architectural dialogue between the two business partners.

The year 1911 saw Wright's return from Europe. His confidence was restored with the publication of a monograph on his work by German publisher Ernst Wasmuth—*Studies and Executed Buildings by Frank Lloyd Wright (Ausgefurhrte Bauten und Entwurfe von Frank Lloyd Wright)*. This publication gave international stature to Wright and was reinforced four years later with the design of the Imperial Hotel in Tokyo, Japan. Meanwhile, commissions in the Midwest were practically non-existent since Wright had become a social outcast. "... And now, alas, he has stepped aside from the right way, left his family and with the wife of another man ... His friends have left him, a great career is blighted, or clients no longer seek him.[11] However, in 1916, Wright's work was once again imprinted on Michigan soil at Grand Beach with the design of three cottages for Chicago businessmen: Joseph Bagley, W.S. Carr, and Ernest Vosburgh who were unconcerned about Wright's controversy. These summer residences Wright designed are smaller adaptations of his Prairie House and probably among the last examples. The Bagley cottage (Fig. 14) is situated high on a bluff overlooking Lake Michigan. It consists of a series of pavilion-like units arranged at right angles allowing for corner windows

Ryerson & Burnham Library, Art Institute of Chicago

Fig. 14. Joseph Bagley cottage, Grand Beach, Michigan, 1916.

on the lake-side. The plan also called for the use of exterior terraces (now enclosed) which connected many of the rooms rather than breaking up the interior space with corridors. This exterior circulation pattern proved problematic during inclement weather. The dwelling also has a floating foundation, similar in principle to the Imperial Hotel, which was designed to counteract earth slippage involving high bluffs along the shores of Lake Michigan. The Carr cottage (Fig. 15) is designed along a longitudinal axis conforming to the configuration of a long, narrow lot. A central corridor, off of which the rooms are placed, bisects the dwelling. Bands of windows, in the Prairie House manner, allow the outside to come in. The Ernest Vosburgh cottage (Fig. 16) extends centrifugally into a wooded setting. The two-story living room is surrounded on three sides by tall vertical windows further integrating the interior with the site. A second floor balcony overlooks the room and the view without:

> ... the breath and boldness of composition curiously formal yet very simple, and the Taliesin-like treatment of the wood and plaster make these among the most agreeable of Wright's smaller houses. The parti of the Vosburgh house resembles that of the Isabel Roberts [River Forest, Illinois, 1908] house while that of the Bagley house has, at much smaller scale, something of the pavilion treatment of the McCormick project [Lake Forest, Illinois, 1907][12]

The Prairie Houses of Frank Lloyd Wright in Michigan represent a major contribution to his work of ''the first golden age.'' The unique design of these dwellings added immensely to the architectural heritage of this Great Lakes state. The architect's later development, a twentieth century architectural manifest destiny, would be enhanced by work he later designed in Michigan.

□ □ □

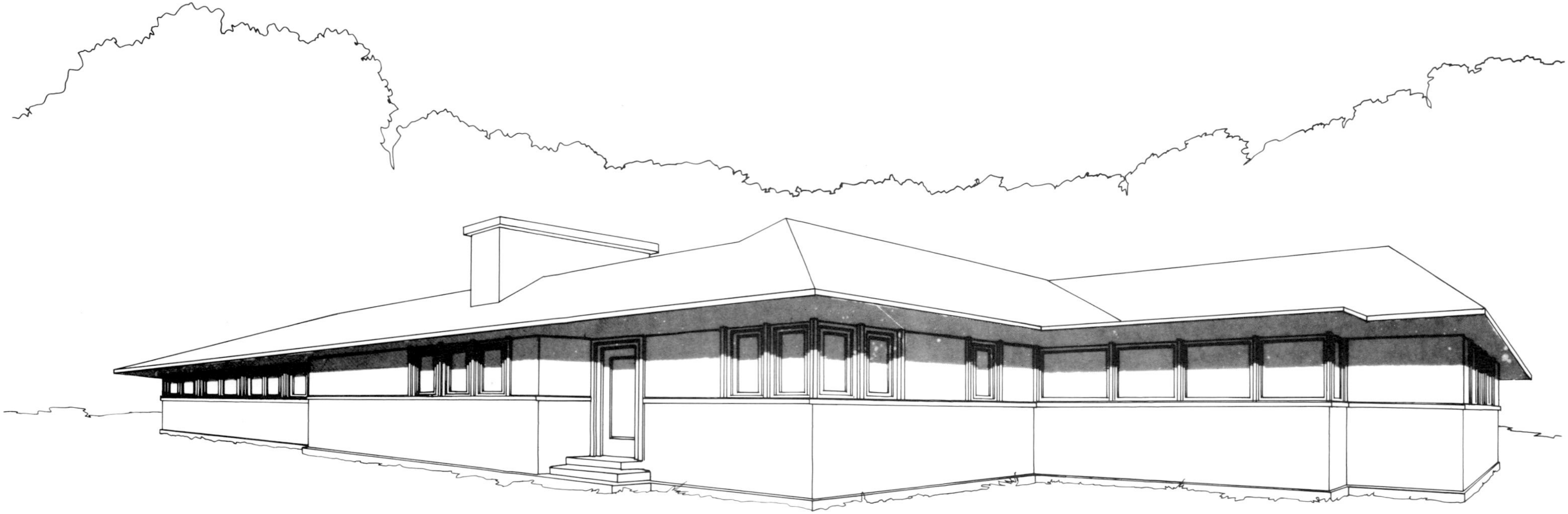

Rendering by Dale Patrick Wolicki

Fig. 15. W.S. Carr cottage, Grand Beach, Michigan, 1916.

Fig. 16. Ernest Voburgh cottage, Grand Beach, Michigan, 1916.

1. Letter, Arthur Heurtley to Oscar Bluemner, July 19, 1908, Archives of American Art, Smithsonian Institution, Washington, D.C.

2. Grant Carpenter Manson, *Frank Lloyd Wright to 1910, The First Golden Age*, Van Nostrand Reinhold, N.Y., 1958, p. 130.

3. Frank Lloyd Wright, *An Autobiography*, Duell, Sloan and Pearce, N.Y., 1943, p. 152.

4. *Notable American Women, The Modern Period*. editors Barbara Sicherman and Carol Hurd Green, Harvard University Press, Cambridge, Massachusetts, 1980, p. 293.

5. H. Allen Brooks, "Frank Lloyd Wright and The Wasmuth Drawings," *Art Bulletin*, June, 1966, p. 194.

6. Wright, p. 162.

7. Manson, p. 213.

8. Robert Lacey, *Ford: The Men and the Machine*, Little, Brown & Company, Boston, 1986, p. 149.

9. Peter Collier and David Horowitz, *The Fords, An American Epic*, Summit Books, N.Y., pp. 70-71.

10. Allan Nevins, *Ford: The Times, the Man, the Company*, Charles Scribner's Sons, N.Y., 1954, p. 227.

11. Letter, Arthur Heurtley to Oscar Bluemner, August 11, 1912, Archives of American Art, Smithsonian Institution, Washington, D.C.

12. Henry-Russell Hitchcock, *In the Nature of Materials: 1887-1941, the Buildings of Frank Lloyd Wright*, Duell, Sloan, and Pearce, 1942, p. 122.

□ □ □

2. The Usonian House

The years 1916-36 could appropriately be dubbed ''a period of transition'' for Frank Lloyd Wright in which he was seeking new frontiers in architecture far away from the controversy his personal life had provoked in the Midwest. Aside from the Imperial Hotel in Tokyo, Japan (1915-22), and his concrete block houses in California (1920-24), ''... this phase of Wright's development is an unfortunate atavism; and it makes more and more pronounced the breach between his work and that which will be pronounced during the coming generation.''[1] Domestic commissions were few and commercial projects never got beyond the drafting table. He commented on this in his autobiography by recalling:

> ... Some further work on the cantilever glass and metal skyscraper for Mr. Johnson [A.M. Johnson, Chicago, Illinois] of the National Life Insurance Company (1924), and a study for the automobile objective for Lawrence Strong (1925) [a planetarium accessible by a spiraling roadway in Sugar Loaf, Maryland], these seem to have ended my active period.[2]

Wright's architectural countenance of character was largely maintained by his public speaking, and publications, which provided him with a source of income. His talks at Princeton University in 1930 were published under the title *Modern Architecture, Being the Kahn Lectures for 1930* by Princeton University Press in 1931. The year 1932 presaged a new beginning with the publication of *An Autobiography* and *The Disappearing City*, as well as founding the Taliesin Fellowship at Spring Green, Wisconsin, his boyhood home:

> Many times before, in desperate circumstances (perhaps because of them) came an Idea. I, too, can get a bad idea - but not this time. The now subjective promise came to its object as the idea? No buildings built at the harrowing moment but, capitalizing thirty-five years of past experience, why not build the builders of buildings against the time when buildings might again be built?[3]

> As the plan for the Taliesin Fellowship unfolded I had hoped that apprentices—like the fingers on my hands—would increase not only my own interest and enthusiasm for my work as an architect, but would also widen my capacity to apply it in the field.[4]

The fellowship was formed in the Fall of 1932 when Wright enlisted the eager, agile hands of architectural apprentices to build a scale model of his utopian vision of the ''new'' American city to be known as Broadacre City. It became a material realization of his attack on what he termed the cultural lag of our society—the city—thus freeing the individual to become self-sufficient on one acre parcels of land in a dwelling designed to be integral with the site. Such an agrarian propriety related to the transcendentalist thought of Ralph Waldo Emerson who Wright greatly admired. Emerson was a believer in the ''divine sufficiency of the individual.''

The year 1936 served to mark Wright's renaissance and ''Second Golden Age'' with the design of the Johnson Wax Administration Buiilding in Racine, Wisconsin for Herbert Johnson; ''Fallingwater'' at Mill Run, Pennsylvania, for Edgar Kaufmann; and the first Usonian House built for Herbert Jacobs in Madison, Wisconsin. The Usonian House was born when Jacobs, a young journalist challenged Wright by asking the architect in 1936 to design a house for him costing five thousand dollars. It was a realistic solution to domestic construction during those difficult economic times. The house utilized low-cost construction techniques: a concrete mat with wrought iron pipes laid underneath for radiant heat; a grid-module plan growing out of a central fireplace and utility core; built-in furniture; and the use of inexpensive building materials assembled on the site helping to defray labor costs. Wright coined the word ''Usonian'' when he was inspired by Samuel Butler's utopian novel *Erewhon*, which is an anagram for ''nowhere.'' If Butler could concoct interesting words in his novel, why not Wright in his own architectural vernacular? He lent credence to his nomenclature by saying, ''... [the architect] must learn ... to fashion his vocabulary for himself and furnish it in a comprehensive way with significant words...[5] Consequently, such words as conglomera, Broadacre, grandomania, and usonian became a working part of the architect's verbal palette. Even one of his apprentices recounted how ''... He loved to play with words, often chose them for sound and not always for sense...

His writing really reflected his speaking—wordy, rich, with a grammar of his own invention.[6]

Although the Herbert Jacobs houses played a paramount role in Wright's re-emergence, there is another significant house Wright designed for Abby Beecher Roberts at Marquette, Michigan, the same year. The house can be traced back to 1935 when Mrs. Roberts' daughter Mary, one of Wright's first apprentices, encouraged her mother to help fund an exhibit of Broadacre City at Marquette. Mrs. Roberts was impressed with some of the model homes in the exhibit and asked Wright to design one for her on a piece of property outside Marquette. The Roberts house (Fig. 17) is a one-story structure based on Usonian principles with a four-foot-square grid-module extending out of a central fireplace. The house is constructed of brick with a raised basement negating the use of radiant heat. The living room and Mrs. Roberts' bedroom both have pitched slab roofs which are among the first designed by Wright. They were necessitated by the heavy winter snowfalls in the upper peninsula of Michigan. Underneath the roofs are tall vertical windows that open the interior to the surrounding woods. The living room and terrace, opposite each other, are arranged at a forty-five degree angle to the central axis of the house.

The original projected cost of the house was $10,000, and ended up being $16,500. It was complicated by one of Wright's apprentices, John Lautner, who was to superintend the construction. When Lautner became Mrs. Roberts' son-in-law, their relationship had some impact on the original plans. Wright pointedly brought this to the attention of Mrs. Roberts:

It was not only ''just a house'' we went in for. But your familiar line was ''I am going to live in it and I don't care to educate myself to new ways of life.'' So where there were idiosyncrasies (they always present themselves as ''common sense'')—idiosyncrasies won... The building of the Marquette house really set him [John] back rather than forward just because he went into residence there (family again) and lost touch with me...[7]

Then Wright went on to further voice his displeasure with John:

Fig. 17. Abby Beecher Roberts house, Marquette, Michigan, 1936.

> I am completely in the dark as to what is going on in connection with our work at Marquette and am beginning to suspect it indiscreet to entrust the Superintendence of a Taliesin project to the son-in-law of a client, even when that son-in-law is you and Mrs. Roberts is the client...[8]

Wright was not in control because he was dealing with a client who was as equally strong-minded and opinionated. That also accounts for the house being listed as ''unsupervised'' in *Frank Lloyd Wright: Writings and Buildings* by Edgar Kaufmann and Sam Raeburn.

Wright's architectural momentum continued to build when he was approached by a group of seven teachers from Michigan State College, the following year, to plan a community of houses for them in Okemos. The houses were arranged around a central farming unit as part of a quasi, self-supporting farming cooperative. It would have become the first small-scale realization of Wright's Broadacre City; however, the project collapsed when the group went to the Federal Housing Authority for financial backing. ''Government expert opinion reported 'the walls will not support the roof; floor heating is impractical; the unusual design makes subsequent sales a hazard,' ''[9] Ironically, five years later Wright was commissioned by the United States government to plan a housing project for defense plant workers in Pittsfield, Massachusetts. As a result of this encounter, federal housing officials also declared that Wright's influence would later become a major one in postwar housing, both public and private.

Undeterred by the Okemos project's failure, two members of the group, Alma Goetsch and Kathrine Winckler, continued on by asking Wright to design a house for them. Winckler wrote to Wright in 1938:

> The idea of having you build a house is not a new one to us. We have talked about it for years, but not until the Jacobs house appeared did we dream that heaven was within reach. I knocked on the door of the Jacobs' house so many times last summer that I finally became apologetic about it. All my life I have resented the little holes in walls that people call windows and as I stood in the Jacobs' bedroom I realiz-

> ed what it must mean to step out of bed in the morning and see earth and trees and sky all at once. I grew up in Madison [Wisconsin) and love hills and water. The knoll on our land seems to be the nearest thing to a hill that can be found hereabouts.[10]

With this statement Winckler reconfirmed all the principles Wright believed in—''The Usonian House aims to be a natural performance, one that is integral with site, to environment, to the life of the inhabitants, integral with the nature of the materials... Into this new integrity, once there, those who live in it take root and grow,,,''[11]

Completed in the fall of 1940, the Goetsch-Winckler house is a visual testament to Wright's Usonian vision. The pronounced horizontality of the house is emphasized by a flat roof defined by fascia lining the perimeter (Fig. 18). Underneath, planes of brick intersect and extend defining the interior and exterior space. The dramatic cantilevered extension of the roof over the carport is re-enforced by the use of a steel beam insuring the horizontal line of the house. With these elements of design and construction there is a marked similarity to the Robie house in Chicago.

Broad expanses of windows open to the east and west integrating the interior with the surroundings and also contributing to the pavilion-like appearance of the house. A second level of clerestory windows wraps around three sides of the living room allowing more light to expand the interior space. Based on Usonian principles, the dwelling rests on a concrete mat, with integral radiant heat, and a four-foot-square module which Wright advocated as the human scale in building proportion. The walls were preassembled utilizing a sandwich technique with an interior core of plywood covered with vapor-lock building paper used as insulation which was then covered with the interior and exterior boards. The ensemble is held together with brass screws. The east side of the house has a span of French doors with one serving as the entry. The framing of the doors serves as vertical counterpoints to the otherwise strong horizontal line of the house.

Although the amount of money Misses Goetsch and Winckler indicated they could afford to pay for the house was $5,000, undoubtedly based on the original projected cost of the Jacobs house, the final cost of the house

Leavenworth Photographics

Fig. 18 Goetsch-Winckler house, Okemos, Michigan, 1939.

was $9,200. This, of course, was a continual problem that confronted many of Wright's projects—cost overruns. However, it didn't thwart the determination of these two devoted clients to live in one of his houses. In those hard economic times Kathrine Winckler borrowed the money from her mother to make the house become a reality.

Wright implicated the builder, Harold Turner:

> ... I am surprised that after giving Turner another chance he would take liberties with the design. We put so much careful study into these little buildings in every detail that it doesn't take much to spoil them for us.[12]

Ann Garrison, one of the original members of the group, remembers being on the site with Turner and observing, ''He would look at Wright's plans and chuckle saying, 'He doesn't mean that;' and scratch it out going on to do something quite different. I think he felt toward Wright that he was a marvelously inspired visionary but that he didn't know much about the practicalities of construction.''[13]

Obviously irritated by Wright's accusation, Misses Goetsch and Winckler responded in a terse letter: ''We are at a loss to comprehend how you arrived at your understanding of what has been done here, since you have neither seen the house or any photographs of it...[14]

And Turner further responded to Wright's accusations with a letter:

> ... After framing the 27 ft. long rafters over the living room, I found it was necessary to double every other one and install a 3/8 x 10 flitch plate. The roof was *first* constructed as shown on the plan but after completion and after the center supports moved away, the center sagged nearly four inches. Yes, the carpentry was and is well done.
>
> This light change is about the only *bad* thing I have done to your house so far—and it works—today the roof has one foot of snow on it and it is still snowing.

> ... It is hard for me to conceive what measure of joy it would bring, if you could translate me into a mere positive person, instead of tossing me relentlessly aside and only reveal me to client after client as something untested and negative ''what a man does, that he has'' and decent, clean, honest and straight work is *my* way to do work as befitteth a man...[15]

Wright was the designer, but Turner was the master-builder who ''took liberties'' to make the house work as a viable structure. In spite of their occasional differences, Wright must have had faith in Turner because he would build two more significant houses for the architect in Michigan.

The confrontation was later mollified when Misses Goetsch and Winckler wrote: ''... We are still making discoveries which amaze us, new patterns of light and shadow... new reasons for blessing the architect who has given us so much joy.''[16] The Goetsch-Winckler house came to be recognized as one of Wright's most gracious, small Usonian Houses.

One of the unbuilt houses for the Okemos group was to be for Alexis Panshin and his family (Fig. 19). Based on the rectangular module, it was designed to have a hexagonal living room area with an extended bedroom wing framed by an open terrace. Mrs. Panshin's observations, upon meeting Wright, provide not only insight into the project but the architect's character as well:

> We became interested through our friendship with several people in the art department at what was then Michigan State College, especially the Brauners.[17] The idea of what Mr. Wright termed Usonia Two had been born, the land bought, a parcel north of the little country road called Mt. Hope, and division had been made when we joined the group. Perhaps we were the last, since we got the area next to the road.
>
> As I recall, we had not yet met Mr. Wright when he designed our house. We visited him later at Taliesin. All I now remember from the visit was his fighting with his sister at the breakfast table over her insistence that a kitchen should NOT be open to the rest of the house,

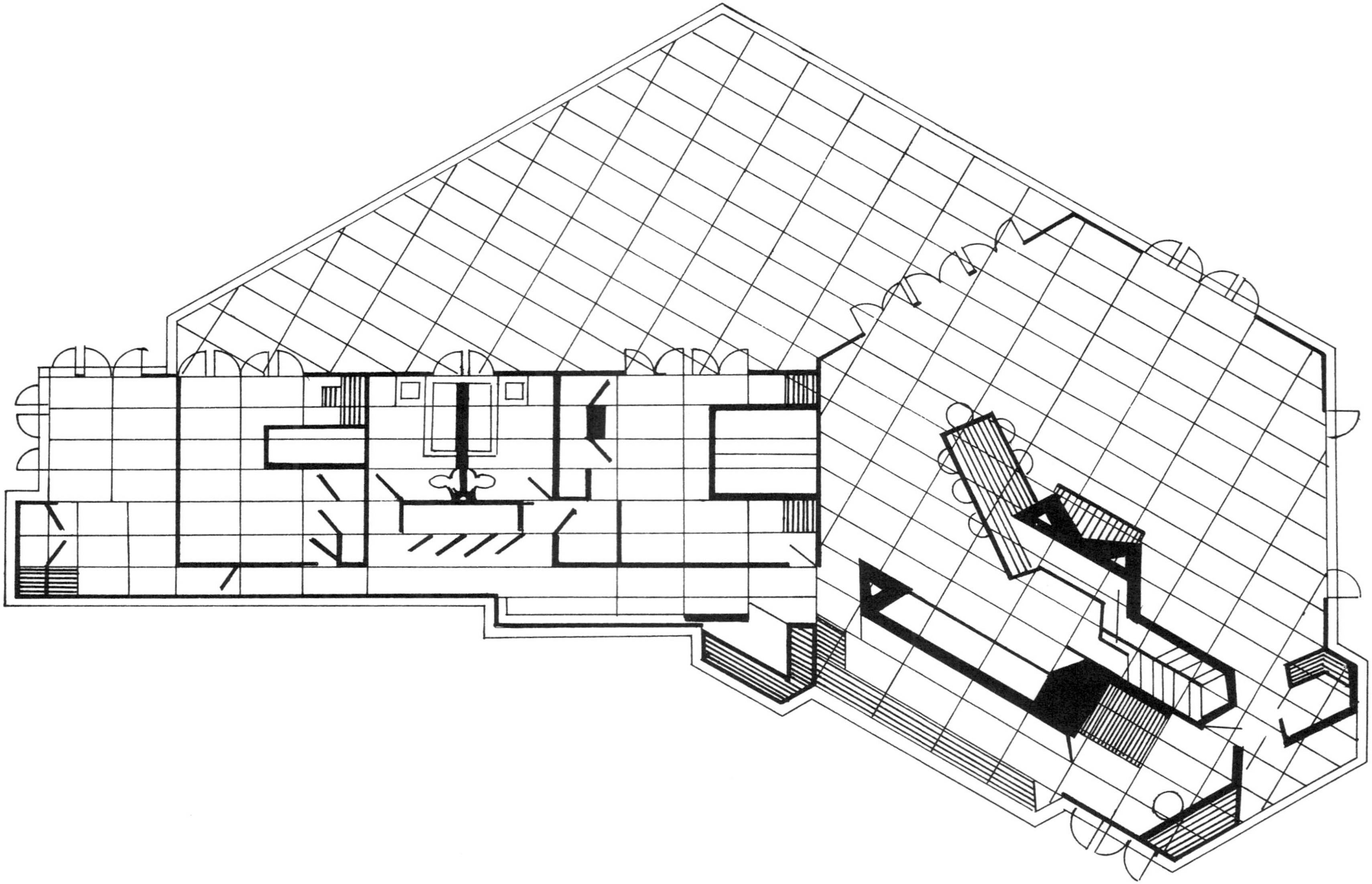

Tom Kettlewell

Fig. 19. Alexis Panshin house, floorplan, Okemos, Michigan, 1937.

> my fascination with his freely using his wide cravat in place of a napkin, and his impatience with consideration of cost as his ideas grew more fanciful. He dreamed of having a zoo inside the circle of houses...[18]

The zoo probably had more to do with farm animals as part of the agrarian character of the community. Wright's disappointment in the failure of the project is revealed in a letter he wrote to Edgar Kaufmann Sr.:

> I hope this letter won't make you mad or anything like that but... I've been driven by the failure of the Lansing group of professors to get money—(seven houses for which we can yet get only 30% preliminary for, although all the plans are made) to see what I can do to tide over the emergency created in the Fellowship by their failure. As one can hope I've been going over the work for you...[19]

With this opening paragraph, Wright then went on to ask Kaufmann for more money because of extra work the fellowship had encountered while building Kaufmann's weekend retreat at Mill Run, Pennsylvania'''Fallingwater.'' Even the big projects which made the small ones possible, were beset with financial problems. Wright was extremely disappointed in the failure of the Okemos project because it would have been the first realization of his Utopian vision—Broadacre City.

□ □ □

1. Lewis Mumford, ''Frank Lloyd Wright and The New Pioneers,'' *Architectural Record,* April, 1929, pp. 414-16.

2. Frank Lloyd Wright, *An Autobiography,* Duell, Sloan, and Pearce, N.Y., 1943, p. 303.

3. Ibid, p. 389.

4. Ibid, p. 399.

5. Frank Lloyd Wright, ''In the Cause of Architecture.'' *Architectural Record,* March, 1908, pp. 4-5.

6. Edgar Tafel, *Years With Frank Lloyd Wright, Apprentice To Genius,* Dover Publications, Inc., N.Y., pp. 134-35.

7. Letter, Frank Lloyd Wright to Abby Beecher Roberts, 11/3/37, courtesy of the Frank Lloyd Wright Archives.

8. Frank Lloyd Wright, *Letters to Apprentices,* edited by Bruce Brooks Pfeiffer, California State University Press, Fresno, CA, 1982, p. 132.

9. ''Frank Lloyd Wright,'' *Architectural Forum,* January, 1948, p. 79.

10. Letter, Alma Goetsch, Katherine Winckler to Frank Lloyd Wright, 10/25/38, courtesy of the Frank Lloyd Wright Archives.

11. Frank Lloyd Wright, *The Natural House,* Horizon Press, N.Y., 1954, p. 134.

12. Letter, Frank Lloyd Wright to Goetsch, Winckler, 3/13/40, courtesy of the Frank Lloyd Wright Archives.

13. Author interview with Ann Garrison, 7/13/90.

14. Letter, Goetsch, Winckler to Frank Lloyd Wright, 7/8/42, courtesy of the Frank Lloyd Wright Archives.

15. Letter, Harold Turner to Frank Lloyd Wright, 1/8/40, courtesy of the Frank Lloyd Wright Archives.

16. Letter, Goetsch, Winckler to Frank Lloyd Wright, 7/28/42, courtesy of the Frank Lloyd Wright Archives.

17. Frank Lloyd Wright designed a house for Erling Brauner in 1946.

18. Letter to author from Mrs. Alexi Panshin, 1/21/85.

19. Frank Lloyd Wright, *Letter to Clients, edited by Bruce Brooks Pfeiffer, Californian State University Press, 1986, p. 106.*

3. Usonian Expansion

In the 1940s, Frank Lloyd Wright expanded upon the design of his Usonian House. Concrete block resurfaced as a building material reinstating what Wright had used on his Los Angeles houses of the 1920s. More attention was given to exterior detail, along with a variety of rooflines, further enriching the Usonian vernacular. Often challenged by the limited budgets of his clients, Wright still managed to produce several outstanding houses in Michigan. They received visual attention in the January, 1948 issue of *Architectural Forum*, featuring Wright's work. The magazine also included two planned communities at Galesburg and Kalamazoo which together became recognized as a modified realization of his Broadacre City project. Other houses Wright designed in Michigan during this decade would make a lasting impression on American domestic architecture.

In 1940, a group of 22 low-income families formed Cooperative Homesteads with the desire to make a post-depression dream become a reality—that of individual home ownership. The group members had earnings too high to qualify for federally subsidized housing but too low to afford the housing they wanted. After seeing the success of some cooperative movements in the United States, the group realized their dream was attainable if they pooled their resources and purchased 120 acres of land in semi-rural Madison Heights outside Detroit. With a pioneering spirit, they planned on building their houses as a group effort. Building materials could be bought collectively to help reduce expenses. The anticipated cost for each house was to be close to $1,600.00. Aaron Green, an apprentice to Wright, had taken leave from the Taliesin Fellowship to study the cooperative movement in the northeastern United States and Canada. He met with the group and encouraged them to enlist Wright as the architect for the project. Thereafter, Green became the supervisor of the project and explained on the building site: "...These are not going to be primitive homes. They are going to include the best of the old traditions, with a natural use of materials. Rather than cover up the physical material, this will be used in the design."[1] The method of construction called for berm-type construction (Fig. 20):

> The berm-type house, with walls of earth, is practical—nice form of building anywhere: north, south, east, or west—depending upon the soil and climate as well as the nature of the site. If your site contains a lot of boulders or rock ledges it is impossible. In the berm-type house the bulldozer comes along, pushes the dirt up against the outsides of the building as high as you want it to go and you may carry the earth banking as far around the structure as you please. Here you have good insulation—great protection from the elements; a possible economy, too, because you do not have to finish any outside below the window level. You do not have to finish the inside walls either if not so inclined. I think it an excellent form for certain regions and conditions. An actual economy and preservation of the landscape.[2]

The origin of berm-type construction can be traced to the treeless plains where it was used by the Mandan and Arikaree Indian tribes of the upper Missouri River region and the Pawnee tribes farther south. There they built villages of huge domelike houses which were buried under a thick mound of hard-packed earth. Later, the early plains settlers adapted sod blocks for house construction much as the eastern frontiersmen had used logs.[3] During his seasonal commutes between Taliesin West in Arizona and Taliesin North in Wisconsin, Wright must have passed through this area and saw some of these sod houses which he deemed a practical form of construction that was indigenous to the area. Subsequently, the berm materialized as a low-cost structural solution for the Cooperative Homesteads project. This same construction technique was used by Wright in the design of the second Herbert Jacobs house in Middleton, Wisconsin (1948) and the Thomas Keys house in Rochester, Minnesota (1951), but the Madison Heights houses were the first.

Construction began by shoveling the earth on the site and packing it into re-usable wooden forms. The composition of the soil was considered ideal, consisting of 70 percent sand and 30 percent clay. The remaining areas, where the dirt had been removed, were planned as sunken gardens that facilitated drainage in a heavy downpour. Concrete piers would support the rafters of the large hip roofs. Modest in size, the houses were planned on a longitudinal axis with a concrete slab and radiant heat, a four-foot square module, central utility core and two bedrooms. One of

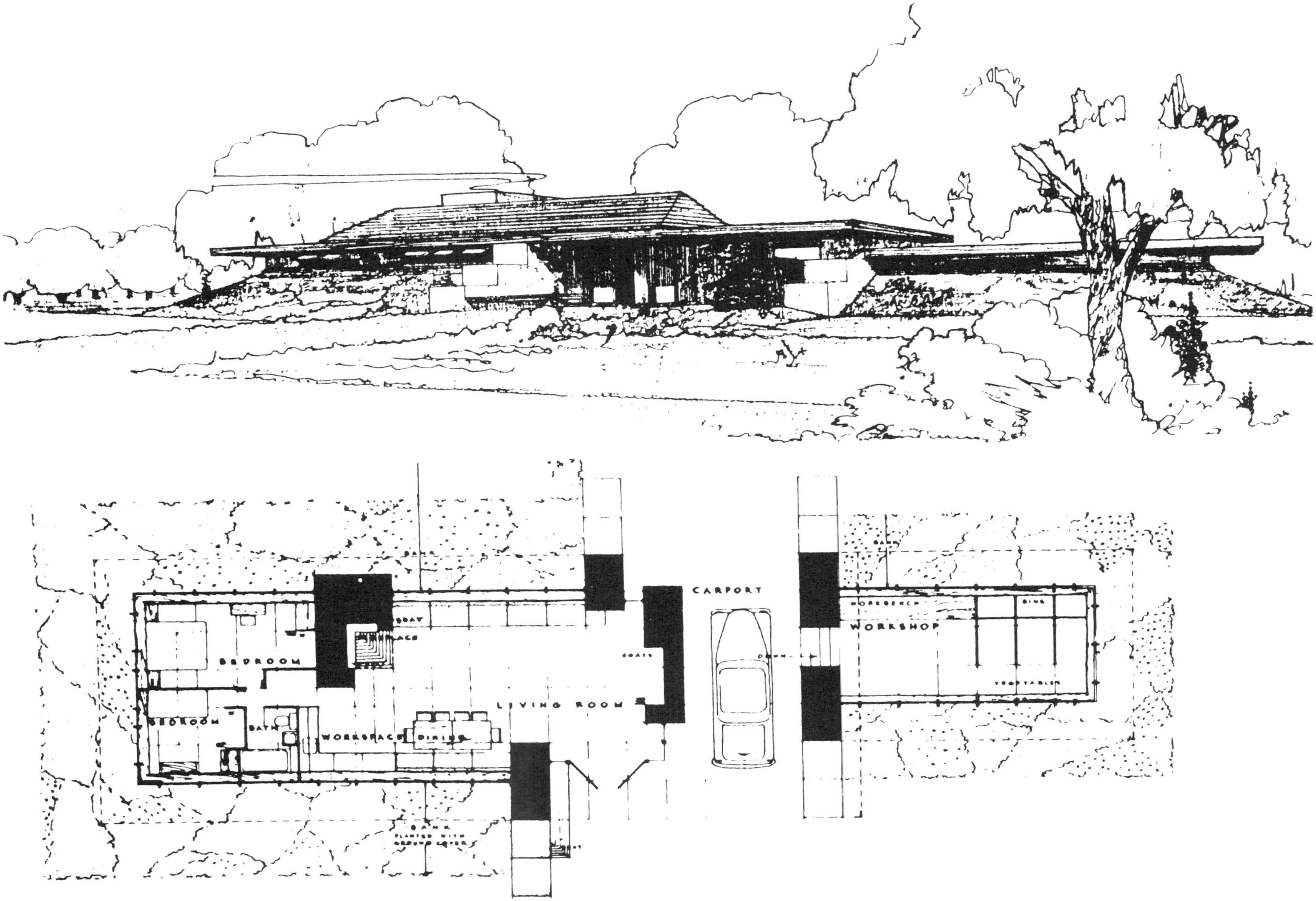

Fig. 20. Cooperative Homesteads project, Madison Heights, Michigan, 1941.

the advantages of the modular-unit system was that it allowed for further expansion while still adhering to the original design.

In a letter dated December 4, 1941, one of the group members, Jim Smith, wrote to Aaron Green that "... It would seem that a workshop in which we can efficiently fabricate our building should receive first consideration, but we will see what is decided at the next meeting, December 7th."[4] That day of infamy marked the United States entry into the Second World War and the ultimate demise of Cooperative Homesteads. Work continued into the fall of 1942 with many of the members working in factories on defense projects; however, they eventually were called off to war and the project collapsed.

The same year as the Cooperative Homesteads venture another project was designed by Wright—a house for Gregor Affleck in Bloomfield Hills. Affleck was born in Chicago and raised in Muscoda, Wisconsin near Wright's homestead in Spring Green. One of Affleck's relatives was a secretary to Wright. These connections helped to nurture a relationship that would subsequently become architect-client. Affleck graduated from the University of Wisconsin in chemical engineering and later migrated to Detroit. In 1940, Affleck asked Wright to design a house for him. As with many other clients, Wright told his client to buy a piece of land nobody else wanted and he would design the house. Thereafter, Affleck purchased several acres of land including a wooded ravine. Wright's plan called for a house that became "of" the site like one of nature's outcroppings.

Construction began in April of 1941 under the supervision of Harold Turner. In a progress report to Wright, Turner wrote:

> ... The Afflecks are thrilled with the progress. Both are inexhaustible admirers of you, your house design and how beautifully the house fits the location.
>
> We have lots of visitors [some of whom were from Cooperative Homesteads] and Mr. Affleck's joy spills over so spontaneously that I believe your name and work is getting in the mind of the total population of the state...[5]

The Affleck house (Fig. 21) typifies the Usonian House with an L-shaped plan defined by a square grid-module and the bedroom wing perpendicular to the living area. It is also termed a ''raised Usonian'' due to a lower level containing a utility area and two small rooms burrowed into the side of the ravine. The living room, on the main level, along with an extending cantilevered deck are supported by I-beams resting on a massive brick pier that anchors the house to the site (Fig. 22). Mr. and Mrs. Affleck saw illustrations of Wright's ''Fallingwater'' in Mill Run, Pennsylvania (1936) and fell in love with its soaring decks and integration with the surroundings. Built out of more natural materials, the Affleck house can be considered a small-scale ''Fallingwater.''

The entry hall, open above with a skylight, leads into the 40-foot long combination living and dining room. French doors define two walls of the living room and open onto the surrounding terrace. The doors are framed by studs four feet on center relating to the four-foot square grid-module. The parapets of the terrace are slanted downward and inward on the outside adding visual interest to the rectilinear lines of the house. Harold Turner, the builder, once again proved himself a master-carpenter as he did with the Goetsch-Winckler house. He carefully mitered and fitted all the cypress boards together much like a cabinet maker. The Affleck house can be considered an architectural tour-de-force of carpentry.

''Nearly ten thousand names appear on the guest register that the Afflecks kept while they lived in the home; they welcomed visitors who wanted to see and talk about the house. 'I'll never forget the morning two busloads of Japanese students knocked on the front door to ask whether they could walk through the house.' said Mary Lutomski [Affleck's daughter].''[6] Turner's observations about visitors during the construction became a daily ritual after the house was completed.

The Affleck house marks a new direction for the Usonian House—one that is grander in scale and proportion for a client beyond moderate means and recalls some of Wright's clients during the ''First Golden Age.''

Also in 1941, Wright designed a house for Carl Wall in Plymouth. Its incubation goes back to Wall's student years at Olivet College. There he

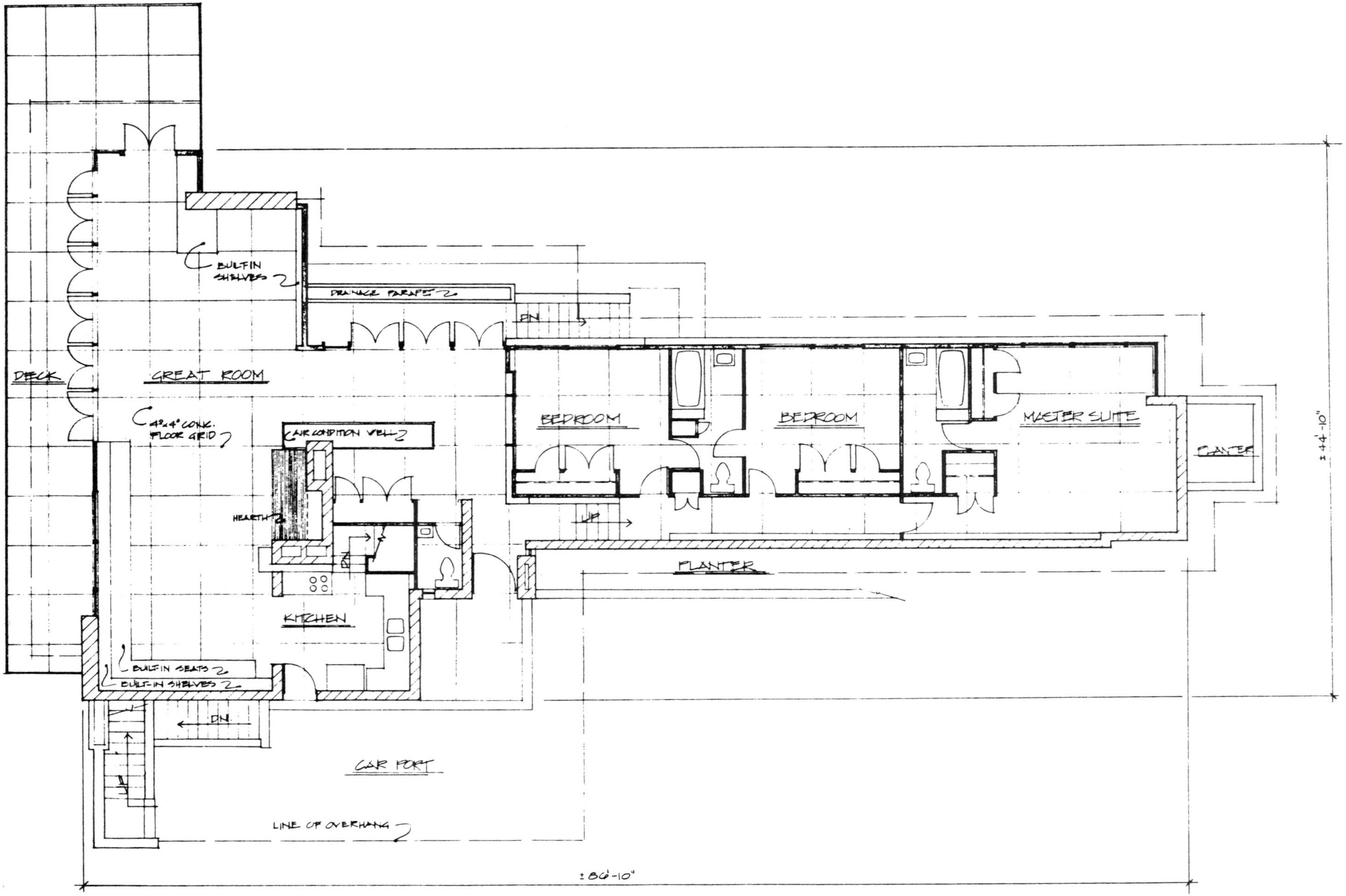

Rendering by Fadi Elchami & Rusty Hudson

Fig. 21. Affleck house, floorplan.

Balthazar Korab

Fig. 22. Gregor Affleck house, Bloomfield Hills, Michigan, 1941.

was introduced to the architect's work by the president of the college, Joseph Brewer, who was a champion of the arts. When Wall was newly married, he expressed a desire to build a Wright house whereupon Brewer took the initiative and wrote a letter to Wright on Wall's behalf. As a result, the Walls were invited to Taliesin to meet with Wright and discuss their plans. Upon their arrival, the architect exclaimed, "Why, your're just children!"[7] Carl was 24, his wife Margaret 22, and Wright 74. Obviously impressed with their youth, Wright included a note with the preliminary plans saying he had "... designed a young romantic house for two young romantic people."[8]

The house Wright planned for the Walls (Fig. 23) blends into the gently rolling landscape. A hexagonal-shaped grass terrace, outside the living room, is supported by an outward slanting brick retaining wall. The wall has a series of horizontal ridges that step up to complement the lines of the house. Built in 1942, it is Wright's first Michigan house based on the diamond-shaped module (Fig. 24). Wright often preferred to incorporate this module into houses built on sloping sites. The projecting angles served to anchor the house to the site by cutting into the landscape. The multiple arrangement of the modules served to form a hexagon incorporating the living room and the kitchen-utility areas as well as defining the guest-servant wing. Wright lent further meaning to these configuarations when he named the house "Snowflake." He said, "Crystals are proof of nature's matchless architectural principle. All this I see as the architect's palette... Materials! What a resource."[9] The Wall house is a materialization of that principle.

Wall originally requested a house costing around $12,000.00. The final figure was between $35,000.00 and $40,000.00 ! Inflated building costs were a problem that beset many of Wright's clients, running two or three times over the original estimates. What did Wright know about building costs? He wasn't a builder; he was an architect. However, with an empathic client like Wall, willing to accept the added costs, the house was built.

In 1946, Wright designed a house for Erling Brauner (Fig. 25) who, like his fellow members of the original Okemos group—Kathrine Winckler and Alma Goetsch—chose to build in the same area. Also based on Usonian

Fig. 23. Carl Wall house, Plymouth, Michigan, 1941.

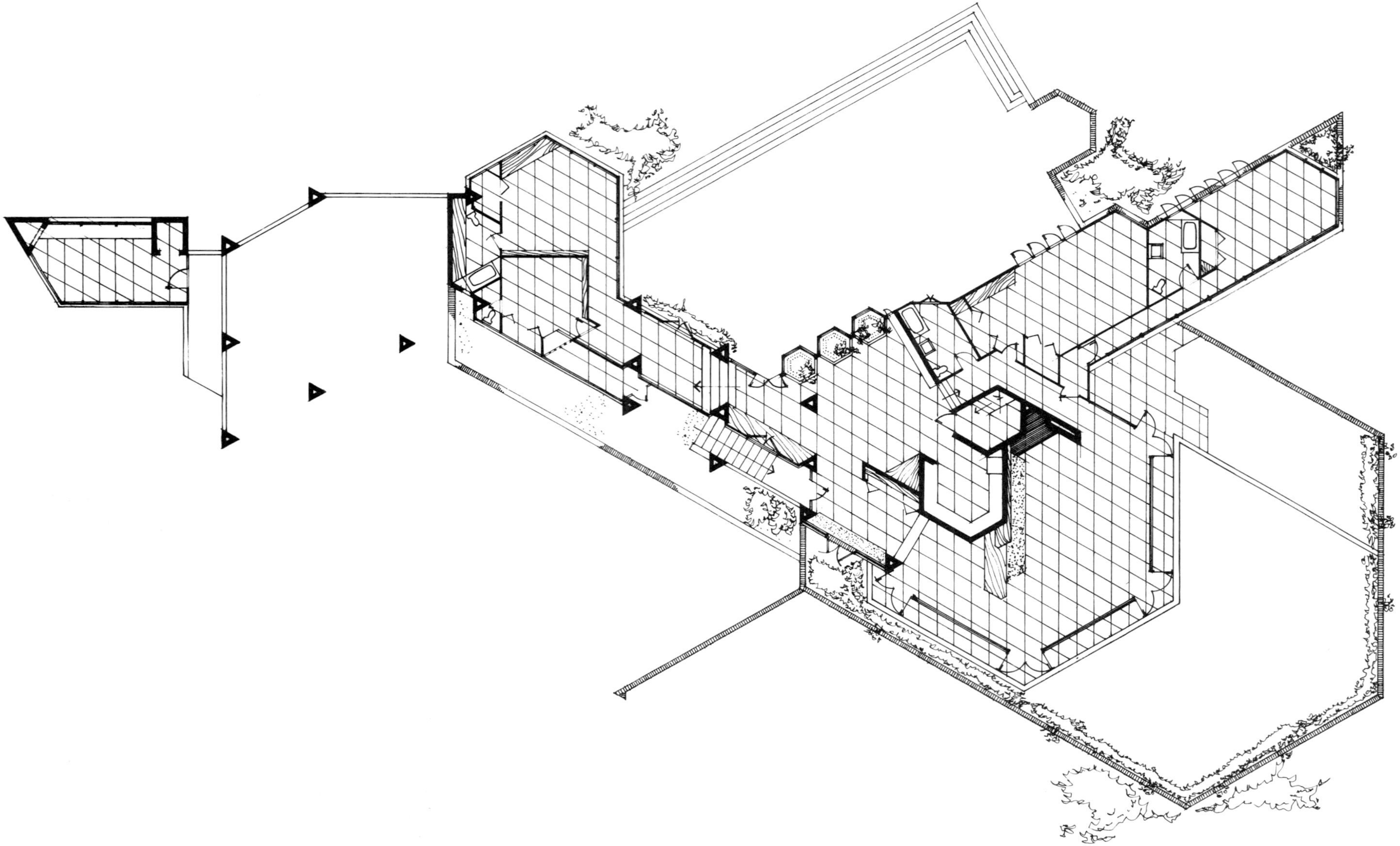

Rendering by Bob Vieracker

Fig. 24. Wall house, floorplan.

principles of design, the Brauner house is a contemporary adaptation of the Prairie House. The floorplan incorporates rectangular modules that define the living area and bedroom wing both of which extend into the landscape. Ribbons of casement windows are placed under the shallow, overhanging hip roof. The house is constructed of commercial concrete blocks. Wright once said to Brauner, ''Let's bring the lowly concrete up out of the basement where it can be seen.'' There are also perforated blocks that were fabricated on the site. They define the wall supporting the roof extension over the carport and also the adjoining wall defining the bedroom hall.

The following year came the Amy Alpaugh house in Northport. The conception of the house goes back to March of 1945 when Wright was invited by fellow architect-friend Eliel Saarinen to give a talk at the Cranbrook Academy of Art in Bloomfield Hills. There Wright invoked his audience to action by saying, ''Work, work, work, night and day.'' Amy, then a student at Cranbrook, was inspired by Wright's philosophy of architecture. She told her mother, who was planning to build a house in Northport, to enlist Wright as the architect. Taking the matter into her own hands, Amy arranged to meet Wright that summer at the Plaza Hotel in New York City where he was doing the preliminary plans for the Solomon Guggenheim Museum. She got lost in the hotel lobby in a maze of mirrors, and finally found Wright as he was stepping off the elevator. He told her she was five minutes late and spoke to her briefly.

Amy followed up with a letter to Wright on June 22, 1945:

> We have property for a home and we would like you to be the architect. The money restrictions are such that we would understand if you didn't accept.
>
> The land is 40 acres in section 28 of Lelanau County, Northport, Michigan. It is one large hill with woods to the north and a beautiful view in the other three directions. To the west is Lake Michigan and the Manitou Islands; south, ten or more miles of rolling farm land; east, Grand Traverse Bay. We are having a roadway built along the west line, through the trees and breaking out on top of the hill.

Fig. 25. Erling Brauner house, Okemos, Michigan, 1946.

> Talking it over we thought it might be better to have two buildings as there are so many things to house. Mother and I would like a studio connected with our bedrooms, hers for weaving and mine for sculpture. Being a prolific person she has two goats and would like to raise chickens. She also enjoys gardening and has in mind a greenhouse. We thought it might be better to divide the house in two parts. One being directly on top of the hill for the living and dining room. That would get the full view with the bedroom studios to the north.
>
> At this time our finances are limited to $7,000. We are willing to sacrifice the main living home for the utility building—animals and such. Then we could save the main house and build it later. We would like plans for both buildings so they will belong together when eventually built.[10]

With this request, Wright designed two dwellings connected by a porte cochere-like structure serving as a covered walkway and entry into a gravel motor court. The design incorporated pitched slab roofs at a thirty degree angle over tall vertical windows lending a dramatic view of the lake in a southern and westerly direction (Fig. 26). The buildings were obliquely arranged to each other because of the topography of the land. Typical of Wright's Usonian Houses, they utilized natural materials of brick with native ash and oak woods, a central fireplace, built-in furniture, and radiant heat under the concrete slab incorporating square modules. The plan for the smaller of the two houses was completed in August of 1947 (Fig. 27) with an estimated cost of $15,000.00. The Alpaughs were obviously undeterred by the five digit number; construction began in the spring of 1948 and the house was completed that fall. The final cost was $47,616.07[11] far exceeding the $7,000.00 the client originally said was available in 1945. One-fourth of the total amount involved carpentry, suggesting a complex structure which took the local carpenters more time to resolve even under the guidance of a Taliesin apprentice. Undoubtedly, the apprentice had little experience in construction—learning the hard way on the job at the owner's expense. With this inexperience, a structural detail must have gone unnoticed as the slab roof blew off in a 60-mile-per-hour gale wind off Lake Michigan leaving Mrs. Alpaugh terrified and helpless when she was

Rendering by Dale Patrick Wolicki

Fig. 26. Amy Alpaugh house, preliminary elevation drawing, Northport, Michigan, 1947.

Fig. 27. Alpaugh house, 1948.

alone in the house. Her son, Bill, in a letter to Wright, dated December 10, 1948, wrote: ''... Corrective measures are imperative before further damage is done...''[12] Wright, on the defensive, wrote back a week later:

> ... Admitting that accidents do happen even in the best regulated families—then think of ours—If the framing had been properly put together I cannot believe the roof would come loose. Out of some 549 structures this is the first time so either there is an extraordinary situation of which we should have been informed or something was lacking in the execution. We are sorry it happened will do what we can to make all secure.[13]

In order to help smooth out the situation, Wright offered to share in the cost of correcting the problem—a first in which he assumed some personal responsibility. It is not surprising that the second building, which would have later functioned as the main house, went unbuilt consumed by the expenses of the first.

During the years of the Second World War, another cooperative group, like the one in Madison Heights, was formed in Galesburg. They were a group of friends, some with the Upjohn Company in Kalamazoo. Realizing they could do better buying land as a group than individually, they pooled their gas ration coupons and drove around the countryside looking for land. Some members of the group, however, felt that Galesburg was too far out and sought land closer to Kalamazoo. In the meantime, Lillian Meyer, one of the members of the Galesburg group, initiated the preliminary stages of their project with a letter to Frank Lloyd Wright at Taliesin in Wisconsin. She wrote on October 29, 1946:

> ...Our group consists of five families who have purchased 71 acres of rolling land... ten miles from downtown Kalamazoo. The surrounding country is similar to yours at Spring Green. We plan to expand eventually to fifteen families.
>
> ... I hope you will be interested in doing our houses and site. We are all enthusiastic and will be keenly disappointed if we can not have a Wright house. I hope we shall hear from you soon.[14]

The following year the splinter group of Galesburg bought 47 acres of land in Kalamazoo to be called Parkwyn village (Fig. 28). They followed the example of Galesburg and also sought Wright to plan their community of homes. The masterplans Wright conceived for the two communities called for the houses to be situated on circular lots with intervening spaces of low growing plants that provided privacy for the residents. The Parkwyn group was later forced to square off their lots when the FHA refused financing for such a radical idea. On November 2, 1947, Wright was invited to give a lecture in Kalamazoo sponsored by the Art Center and the Galesburg and Parkwyn groups. To an audience of over 1,000 people, he espoused his philosophy of architecture and how it can affect the lives of people with a ''new harmony within ourselves'' and ''a different way of thinking about life.'' Coincidentally the same attitude was taking place in the lives of the members at Galesburg-Parkwyn—a new way of living.

The amount of money the members felt they could afford to pay for their houses at Galesburg and Parkwyn was $12,000.00; however, when Wright sent the preliminary drawings for the first houses to be built, his estimated cost was $20,000.00. This provoked one of the members who wrote to Wright saying: ''They are rich man's houses and far beyond our means.'' The matter was resolved with a figure of $15,000.00 by using concrete block in the construction. Member participation in building the houses also served to reduce the building costs. This experience serves to qualify the extent of Wright's involvement in many of his projects. He not only designed the houses, but was expected to come up with reasonable building cost estimates, and, when deemed too expensive to find a solution to reduce them. This is one of the unrecognized features that characterized Frank Lloyd Wright—an architect of design ingenuity, and, sometimes cost analyst. In order to enhance the nondescript concrete block to be used, the group decided they wanted to incorporate textile design into blocks. After visiting Wright at Taliesin West, Robert Levin, Secretary of the Parkwyn group, wrote:

> ...On my return those of us who are working together on the textile blocks got together to discuss the current status of our project. We decided that it would help us greatly to have examples of the molds

Frank Lloyd Wright Archives

Fig. 28. Frank Lloyd Wright at Parkwyn Village with Robert Levin and David Weisblat, May 25, 1949.

> used on the Florida Southern [College] buildings [begun in 1940], so that we could get our special molds built faster. We believe we have a good mold for the standard blocks, and are obtaining bids for its construction.[15]

Construction began in the spring of 1949 on the first houses: Robert Levin and Ward McCartney at Parkwyn; Samuel Eppstein, Eric Pratt, and David Weisblat at Galesburg. The Levin, McCartney, and Weisblat houses are based on the L-shaped Usonian plan whereas the Pratt and Eppstein houses are longitudinal. The houses have different rooflines: Eppstein and Pratt are flat; McCartney and Weisblat hipped; and Levin has a pitched slab. The grid-module design, allowed for later additions to accommodate growing families. The Levin house (Fig. 29), built first, rests on a gently sloping hill with a projecting living room framed by a pitched slab roof and tall vertical windows oriented to the view. A raised terrace outside the living room has a screened enclosure which Wright originally opposed. ''Use more fly spray,'' he said, yet later acquiesced with a design for an enclosure made out of plumbing pipe. The Ward McCartney house (Fig. 30) is perhaps the most dramatic Usonian House designed by Wright at Parkwyn Village. The shallow hip roof has acute 14-degree angles that make up the roof pitch on two of the three corners of the house. It is the second Usonian House in Michigan to use the diamond-shaped module. One razor-sharp eave is cantilevered 18 feet, from heel to toe, almost attempting to touch the adjoining slope. Due to the acute angles and unsupported weight, the roof of the house began to disengage itself from the utility core. McCartney, a dentist, was literally trying to keep a roof over his head while building up a practice. The matter was resolved with steel cables tying the rafters to the central core.

Like Parkwyn, the design emphasis of the houses at Galesburg is on horizontality relating them to their sites. The plan of the Samuel Eppstein house follows a longitudinal axis which extends outward to become a raised, circular grass terrace supported by a concrete block wall. The abstract design of the perforated textile blocks on the Eppstein house is a variegated play of horizontal lines (Fig. 31). The wide fascia of overlapping boards on the Pratt house (Fig. 32) is complemented by bands of windows underneath, together creating a strong horizontal composition.

Fig. 29. Robert Levin house, Kalamazoo, Michigan, 1948.

Fig. 30. Ward McCartney house, Kalamazoo, Michigan, 1949.

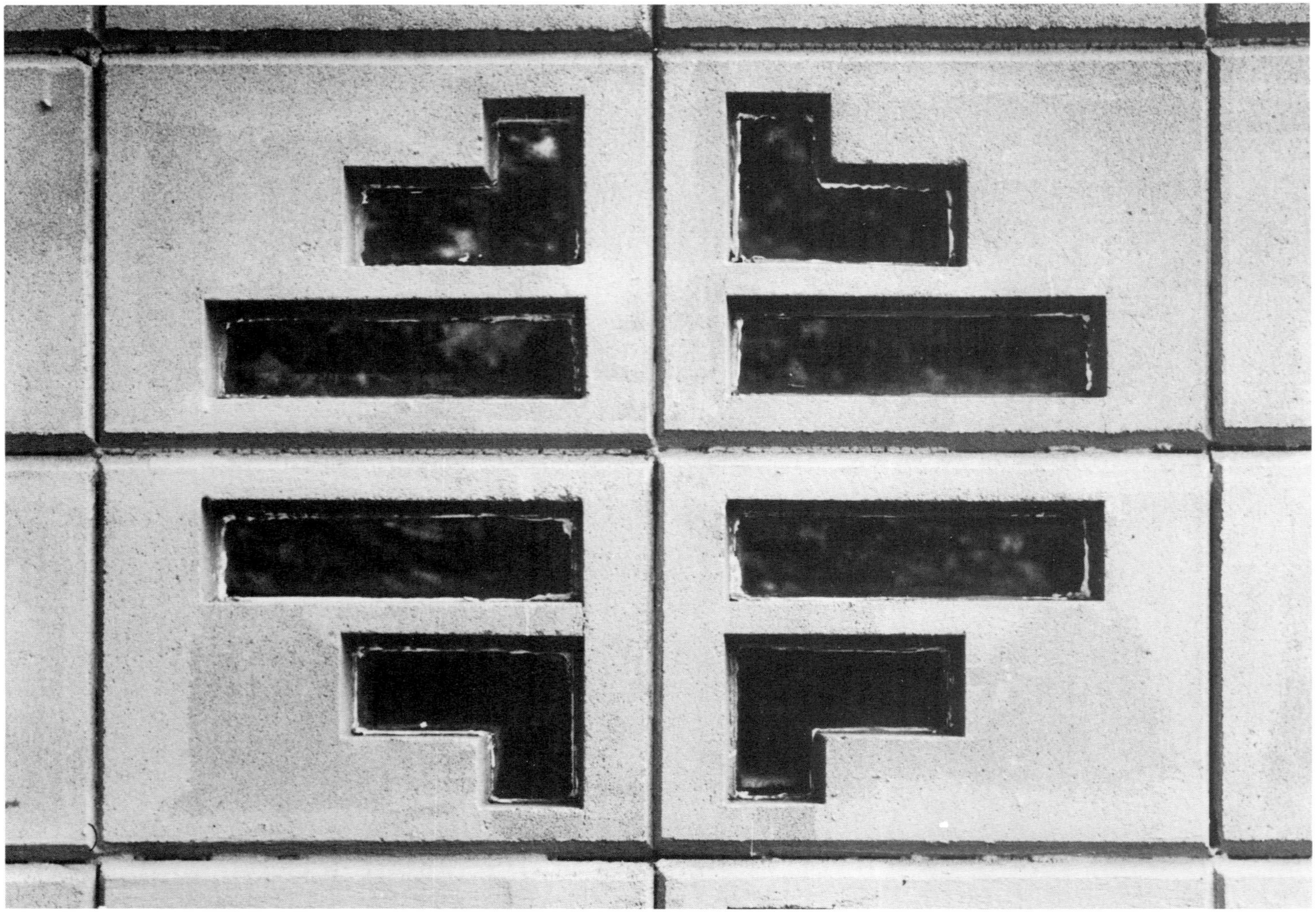

Fig. 31. Samuel Eppstein house, detail of block, Kalamazoo, Michigan, 1948.

A second roof defines the projecting living-dining area that intersects with the longitudinal axis of the bedroom wing. Here the interpenetration of masses recalls Wright's Prairie Houses of ''the First Golden Age.'' The David Weisblat house (Fig. 33) is burrowed into a slope with the roof almost touching the ground and makes the structure look like it is growing out of the site.

The Galesburg and Parkwyn projects became small-scale realizations of Wright's Broadacre City of 1932:

> He imagined man living on spacious land in the forests, meadows, hills and prairies but gathering in park-like central areas for work, play, and study. The freedom provided by the automobile would allow him to live in close contact with nature and yet work in convenient centralized areas... He planned for each citizen spacious acreage, in which healthy living and exposures to nature's beauty would encourage a new American culture.[16]

William Wesley Peters, vice-president of the Frank Lloyd Wright Foundation, in a tribute to the Galesburg-Parkwyn groups, said, ''... These two projects were always dear to Frank Lloyd Wright and the fact that through the concerted efforts of respected individual clients the projects actually came into being meant much to him.[17] Wright's Broadacre City was finally realized in Michigan.

In September of 1946, Melvyn Maxwell Smith commissioned Frank Lloyd Wright to design his new home in Bloomfield Hills. Such an endeavor dates back to Smith's college days when he saw examples of the architect's work in a humanities class. His enthusiasm had been picqued and he later found examples in the January, 1938 issue of *Architectural Forum* devoted to the creative efforts of Wright in the mid-thirties. Also, ''... It was filled with quotations from Thoreau and Whitman and others who were prime motivators of the Master's psyche.''[18] One quotation by Thoreau served as a primary source of inspiration and motivation to Smith—''A rich man is he whose needs are few.'' These words could be used as a literary metaphor applicable to Wright's modest-size Usonian House—one that Smith would build for himself. In December, 1946, he received the general

Fig. 32. Eric Pratt house, Galesburg, Michigan, 1948.

plans and drawings followed by the working plans in June, 1947. Afterwards, Smith received building estimates and found they were three or four times over Wright's estimate. Discouraged by the possibility of not seeing his dream become a reality, he went to Wright explaining the setback. The architect advised Smith to become his own contractor with the advantage of buying materials at cost. Subsequently, following Wright's suggestion, he studied the plans for two years in order to familiarize himself with the rudiments of building. Construction of the house began in 1949 and was completed in 1950.

The Smith house (Fig. 34) is a reworking of the Herbert Jacobs house (1936). It is L-shaped with the living and bedroom wings defined by a rectangular grid-module extending out from the utility core. Unlike the more modest Jacobs house, the details of the Smith house are richer. The canted fascia

Balthazar Korab

Fig. 33. David Weisblat house, Galesburg, Michigan, 1949.

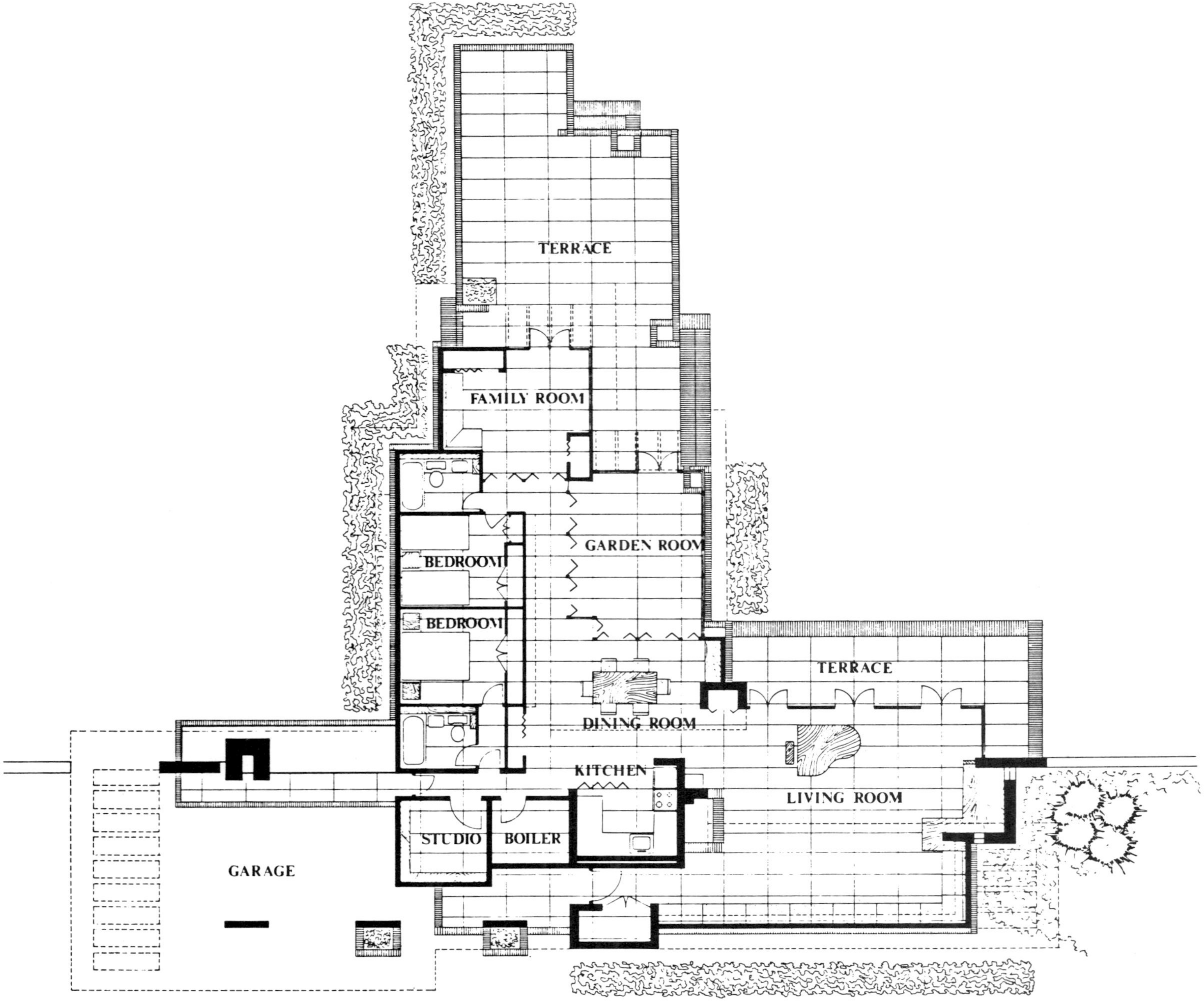

Rendering by Marie Garcia & Rosalind Tieleman

Fig. 34. Melvyn Maxwell Smith house, floorplan, Bloomfield Hills, Michigan, 1946.

Fig. 35. Smith house, front.

Fig. 36. Smith house, detail of rear.

boards have a projecting belt course of corbels and the eaves a trellis configuration with inset lights (Fig. 35). Patterned, perforated boards are used for the clerestory windows on the north side of the structure which is tucked into a hillock (Fig. 36) serving as an insulation barrier in winter. When Smith was initially examining the elevation drawings with Wright at Taliesin North, he noticed that the second level of clerestory windows, on the front of the house, terminated at the utility core. He pointed this out to Wright by asking, ''Why not continue the windows through the core?'' Wright stood for a minute, tapping his pencil on the drafting board, and turned to Mrs. Smith commenting, ''Your husband would have made a fine architect.''[19] This is one of the few times when a client of Wright collaborated on the design of his own house. There was a camaraderie between Wright and Smith that was long lasting, as there was with many other Michigan clients establishing a symbiotic relationship that encouraged a Usonian expansion.

□ □ □

1. *The Detroit News,* October 11, 1942, p. 18.

2. Frank Lloyd Wright, *The Natural House,* Horizon Press, N.Y., p. 148.

3. Glen Rounds, *The Treeless Plains,* Holiday House, N.Y., p. 30.

4. Letter, Jim Smith to Aaron Green, December 4, 1941, courtesy of the Frank Lloyd Wright Archives.

5. Letter, Harold Turner to Gregor Affleck, May 30, 1941, courtesy of the Frank Lloyd Wright Archives.

6. *The Frank Lloyd Wright Newsletter,* March-April, 1978, The Frank Lloyd Wright Association, Oak Park, Illinois, p. 2.

7. Carl Wall, ''A Visit With Frank Lloyd Wright,'' paper dated January 21, 1986.

8. Carl Wall, ''Frank Lloyd Wright Houses in Michigan,'' paper for a Michigan history at Eastern Michigan University, November 21, 1979.

9. Edgar Kaufmann (ed.), *An American Architecture: Frank Lloyd Wright*, Horizon Press, N.Y., 1955, p. 96.

10. Letter, Amy Alpaugh to Frank Lloyd Wright, June 22, 1945, courtesy of Frank Lloyd Wright Archives.

11. Cost account of ''Northport Cherry Farm,'' courtesy of Amy Alpaugh Russell.

12. Letter, Bill Alpaugh to Frank Lloyd Wright, December 10, 1948, courtesy of Frank Lloyd Wright Archives.

13. Letter, Frank Lloyd Wright to Bill Alpaugh, December 18, 1948, courtesy of Amy Alpaugh Russell, courtesy of Frank Lloyd Wright Archives.

14. Letter, Lillian Meyer to Frank Lloyd Wright, October 29, 1946, courtesy of the Frank Lloyd Wright Archives.

15. Letter, Robert Levin to Frank Lloyd Wright, June 2, 1949, courtesy of The Frank Lloyd Wright Archives.

16. Lovanna Lloyd Wright, *Architecture: Man in Possession of His Earth, Frank Lloyd Wright*, Doubleday & Co., Garden City, N.Y., 1962, p. 119.

17. Letter, William Wesley Peters to Western Michigan Chapter, AIA, December 13, 1984.

18. *The Frank Lloyd Wright Newsletter*, March-April, 1978, The Frank Lloyd Wright Association, Oak Park, Illinois, p. 5.

19. Author interview with Melvyn Maxwell Smith, summer, 1979.

4. Efflorescence

When Dwight D. Eisenhower became the 34th president of the United States in 1953, one Pennsylvania housewife said, ''It's like America has come home.'' Prior Republican partisans of Howard Taft for president responded to the Eisenhower victory by saying, ''It looks like he's pretty much for home, mother, and heaven.'' So too was Frank Lloyd Wright for the home by continuing his ''Usonian Manifest Destiny.'' When designing one of his houses on the drafting board at Taliesin, Wright began to draw outside his usual grid-module design. One of his apprentices observed, ''Mr. Wright, you just went off the grid,'' and he replied, ''I''m not going to be a slave to the grid just because I invented it.''[1] In 1953, The National Association of Home Builders lent further credence to the impact of the Usonian House with a ''Trade Secrets'' house displayed in 15 cities. It was designed to meet the burgeoning demand for post-war housing. The public response was overwhelming with people liking the open kitchen; extreme simplicity with low, long lines of a shallow pitched roof; small bedrooms; storage walls; and a carport. These design elements had become a national Usonian diffusion that penetrated the minds of Wright's Michigan clients.

One such client was James Edwards who was drawn to the work of Frank Lloyd Wright when he read an article by Loren Pope titled ''The Love Affair of A Man and His House'' in the August, 1948 issue of *House Beautiful*. Wright had designed a small Usonian House for Pope at Falls Church, Virginia in 1940. Perhaps Edwards was moved when he read:

> ...It is the only kind of habitation fit for man because it has a presence and a soul. Why? First, because it is a work of principle. And the other reasons grow out of the first. Because it is a work of principle, it is honest and being honest, it is both eloquent and quiet. Buildings are close to our lives and influence them, consciously or unconsciously. Mr. Wright's buildings are a tangible expression of his philosophy. He thinks America is synonymous with freedom...[2]

Seeking a new house, also based on principle, Edwards wrote to Wright on August 2, 1948:

> ... Although it may be preposterous to assume that we can enjoy a Frank Lloyd Wright home, I believe that we will never allow ourselves to follow the usual dull plan and methods of home construction.
>
> Some of the dissatisfaction with orthodox building comes from my work. I am the manufacturing methods engineer for Oldsmobile. Our assignment is to develop new and better ways of making things—without complete regard to conventional production practices. We usually find that when we get back to the basic facts—better methods are not difficult to develop.
>
> Our thinking on home building follows the same line. We would like to forget the usual house construction and start with the theory that our home can play with us, and work with us if we will let it—if we can get your help ...[3]

Edwards met with Wright shortly thereafter to discuss his plans. Afterward he bought a piece of rolling, wooded land in Okemos not too far from the Goetsch-Winkler house which he went to see. There he discussed Wright's work with Alma Goetsch. Edwards was so thorough in his examination of the property he bought that he offered to send Wright a 16mm film of the site. The preliminary drawings arrived in April of 1949 with Edwards responding: "The house is a masterpiece—Perfect in every way. We would like you to proceed with the working drawings."[4]

The house, completed in 1952 (Fig. 37), is an L-shaped Usonian with the living room growing out of the central utility core at an oblique angle. Resting on a canted brick base, with a series of setbacks, the house appears to grow out of the sloping site. The plan incorporates a square grid-module unlike the diamond module often used by Wright on similar topographical sites. The angle of the living room allows for windows on three sides opening the interior to a view of the woods beyond. The bedroom wing has French doors which lead out onto a terrace. Like all of Wright's Usonian Houses, the design is oriented to the out-of-doors. As Wright once said, "The building ends where nature begins, and nature

Wayne Andrews

Fig. 37. James Edwards house, Okemos, Michigan, 1949.

ends where the house begins.'' There is a total integration of the Edwards house with the site.

In January, 1949, Howard Anthony wrote to Frank Lloyd Wright asking the architect to design a house for him in Benton Harbor. Because Anthony was a mechanical inventor of electronic equipment, he undoubtedly was visually receptive to the unique design of Wright's architecture. Thereafter, he followed up with a more detailed, three-page letter outlining his space requirements including a small electrical laboratory to work in. ''... We have felt for many years that we would like a house designed by you, as your houses seem to express most nearly what a house should be ...''[5] Completed in 1950, the Anthony house (Fig. 38) has a shallow hip roof 50 percent larger than the enclosed areas. The overhangs vary from three feet to ten feet the latter of which is reinforced with a steel beam. Based on the L-shaped plan, with a diamond grid-module, the house exterior is finished with Wisconsin limestone and cypress. The diamond module helps to compile acute and obtuse angles both inside and outside the house. The stonework has a marked resemblance to Wright's home in Spring Green, Wisconsin. The architect had this in mind when he specified: ''... Stone ... would be a broken range random ashlar with occasional projecting courses as at Taliesin. Horizontal joints raked 3-4'' deep; vertical joints flush.''[6] The masonry walls rise to a common sill height topped with ribbons of windows. The shallow hip roof shelters the structure and the massive chimney anchors it to the dramatic site. Obviously pleased with the results, Anthony wrote to Wright:

> Neither [Mrs. Anthony] nor I is very competent at expressing our pleasure. However, we do want you to know that you have interpreted our wishes far better than we had hoped, and we really feel that you have designed for us the most beautiful house you have yet produced. The manner in which you have exactly provided the things we wanted and yet did not mention to you seems almost unbelievable.[7]

Near the Anthony house, in neighboring St. Joseph, Wright planned a house, built in 1950, for Ina Morriss Harper. The origin of the project involved the same set of circumstances as James Edwards. Harper had also

Ezra Stoller, Esto Photographics

Fig. 38. Howard Anthony house, Benton Harbor, Michigan, 1948.

read the article in *House Beautiful* magazine by Loren Pope. Afterward, she too was inspired and wrote to Wright in November of 1948:

> Until I read ''The Love Affair of A Man and His House,'' by Loren Pope, in *House Beautiful,* I had thought a house designed and built upon the principles of Mr. Wright could be only a dream for many years.
>
> May I ask how one may build such a house?
>
> My husband and I have a lot which overlooks Lake Michigan which is roughly triangular in shape ... We wish to build a five room ''ranch type'' house of approximately twelve to thirteen hundred square feet ...[8]

Eugene Masselink, Wright's secretary, followed up with a letter specifying the physical requirements Wright needed before he would accept a commission. Harper responded:

> ... I note that ''Dwelling-houses upon urban lots will not be accepted.'' The lot upon which we wish to build is within the city limits of St. Joseph, Michigan and is supplied by city utilities. The neighborhood is secluded. I enclose a sketch of the lot in the hope that its position on the bluff overlooking Lake Michigan will offset the size of the building site and make the location sufficiently interesting for Mr. Wright's consideration.[9]

Wright subsequently accepted the project and designed a very dramatic house obliquely sited on a corner lot taking advantage of the lake view beyond. The house (Fig. 39) was developed along two axes crossing at 45 degree angles. The open living, dining and work areas grow out of a central fireplace which has always served as the ceremonial symbol of domesticity in a Wright house (Fig. 40). The cypress ceiling and salmon colored brick walls contrast with the polished concrete floor mat with a square grid-module. Tall vertical windows, under a pitched slab roof, open onto the terrace and the lake view beyond. Built-in furniture is integral with the interior which, in turn, is integral with the site. Abutting the slab roof, that defines the living area, is a shallow hip roof over the adjoining bedroom wing. Among the several gracious, small Usonian Houses Wright designed in Michigan, the Harper house suitably blends into the site while opening to the view of Lake Michigan.

Wayne Andrews

Fig. 39. Ina Morris Harper house, St. Joseph, Michigan, 1950.

Ezra Stoller, Esto Photographics

Fig. 40. Harper house, interior of living room.

The Eric Brown house (Fig. 41), in Parkwyn Village, was designed by Wright in 1950 and completed in 1952. It has a longitudinal axis under a continuous gabled roof accentuating the horizontal flow of the house. The deep overhangs of the roof help to create a sense of shelter which was always an important part of Wright's design dating back to the Prairie House. The masonry blocks comprise a series of intersecting planes defined by the square module. This is considered a trademark of Wright's architecture comparable to sculpture—the interpenetration of form and space. The living room has the conventional French doors opening out onto the terrace. On the opposite side of the house a band of small window perforations in the wall define the gallery leading to the bedrooms while providing privacy from the adjacent road. The dwelling can be considered

Ezra Stoller, Esto Photographics

Fig. 41. Eric Brown house, Kalamazoo, Michigan, 1950.

Fig. 42. Robert Winn house, Kalamazoo, Michigan, 1950.

two-faced: open to nature on one side, closed on the other, yet both defining the living space within. Also designed the same year in Parkwyn is the Robert Winn house (Fig. 42). It rests on the side of a hill and could be termed a raised Usonian, similar to the Affleck house, because of a lower level. The end of the dwelling has a series of setbacks with corner windows dissolving the mass of the house. On the adjacent side a semi-circular porch is oriented to the view of a small lake beyond. The house is compatible with the site and met the moderate cost projected for the client.

The Curtis Meyer house (Fig. 43) at Galesburg was also planned by Wright in 1950 and based on the solar hemicycle design of the second Herbert Jacobs house in Middleton, Wisconsin (1944). Wright referred to this scheme as a ''real first.'' The radiating, rectangular modules of the house were determined by six-degree sectors of a circle. Fifteen sectors define the quarter-circle configuration of the Meyer house. Mahogany mullions support the 14-feet high windows which are two sectors wide. The vertical expanse is broken by a horizontal lintel supporting the clerestory window above. The projecting, curved eaves are cantilevered on the ends almost attempting to complete the circle. A convex seating area in the living room faces the fireplace. The second floor bedroom area overlooks the living room and is separated by a low parapet clad with beveled mahogany boards. The forms and spaces work together like clockwork. Unlike the other houses in Galesburg and Kalamazoo, fabrication of the concrete blocks would have been too problematic because of the house curvature. Commercial blocks were used instead. As a result, the vertical joints of the blocks on the convex walls were too broad necessitating gunnite for filler. The floorplan is an interesting interplay of curvilinear lines undoubtedly inspired by the Guggenheim Museum design built nine years later.

Along with the Meyer house, Wright also designed a house for William and Mary Palmer in Ann Arbor the same year. It is the consummate realization of a Wright house that is ''of the hill rather than on it.'' The initial conception of the house, often recounted by Wright clients, is best told by Mary Palmer:

> ''Why did you choose Frank Lloyd Wright as your architect?'' This invariably is the first question asked by a visitor to our home in Ann

Fig. 43. Curtis Meyer house, Galesburg, Michigan, 1950.

> Arbor. Our answer takes us back to our purchase ... of a building site adjacent to the arboretum in the hilly section between the city and the Huron River. For the next two years we busied ourselves in the architectural library reading magazines and books, studying photographs and plans and even attempting some amateur designing of our own. The more we studied and observed trends in home design the more interested we became in the ideas and achievements of Frank Lloyd Wright. Finally, after spending an hour in the Gregor Affleck house, designed by Mr. Wright, in Bloomfield Hills, we came out simultaneously with identical statements, "Let's try to get Mr. Wright."[10]

The Palmers were impressed with the interplay of cypress, brick, glass and the deep red leather-like concrete floors. "We allowed our eyes to move to a band of windows opposite—and on—to the outside bare trees. Moving nearer the windows, we saw the ravine below."[11]

The hilly location of the Palmer house once again dictated the use of the diamond grid-module (Fig. 44). Wright also varied the floor level further making the house compatible with the site. The original plan arranged the house so the terrace, off the living room, overlooked the road below. The Palmers were not amenable to the idea, preferring more privacy. Consequently, they placed a silhouette of the house on a topographical map, orienting the terrace to the yard at the back of the lot, and sent it to Wright. He accepted the overture reinforcing his receptivity to clients' participation in the design process. Access to the front door is by a ritual-like entry of gently rising stairs. The wall, flanking the stairs, has perforated blocks with inset glass allowing light to filter into the kitchen behind. The living room cypress-wood ceiling is pyramidal sheltering the interior space. Outside, a 24-foot extension of the living room roof over the terrace serves to mediate the interior and exterior spaces. The Palmer house is one of Wright's more elegant Usonian Houses in Michigan and a visual testament to the marriage of a house with its site.

When the James Edwards house was being built in 1950, Donald Schaberg, a friend of Edwards, became enamored of Wright's architecture during construction. Consequently, he commissioned Wright to plan his house,

Balthazar Korab

Fig. 44. William Palmer house, Ann Arbor, Michigan, 1950.

also in Okemos. The plan of the Schaberg house, like the Brown house in Kalamazoo, follows a longitudinal axis. Wright often did variations on the same theme taking into consideration the individual needs of his clients. The Schaberg house has an extended gabled roof, with six-foot eaves on each end, accentuating its horizontality. The plaster ceiling of the living room follows the two planes of the roof to a height of 12 feet at the ridge of the interior. This choice of material was largely necessitated by the high cost of cypress and mahogany wood often specified for interior finishing. Plaster ceilings became characteristic of Wright's later Usonian Houses. The four-foot soffits outside, also covered with plaster, visually integrate the exterior and interior spaces. Bands of windows, on two sides of the living room, lend a sense of buoyancy to the ceiling (Fig. 45). Wright, as in all his buildings, has created a sense of space which liberates the house from any confining features. This idea was further reinforced by a talk Wright gave the same year:

> ... That primitive sense of shelter is a quality architecture should always have. If in a building you feel not only protection from above, but liberation of interior to outside ... then you have one important secret of letting the interior space come through.[12]

The circumstances surrounding the Lewis Goddard house in Plymouth, designed by Wright in 1952, are similar to those of the Schaberg house. Goddard was a close friend of Carl Wall and observed the construction of the Wall house. Consequently, he approached Wright to design a house to be built on seven and a half acres next to the Wall property. The Goddard house is typically Usonian (Fig. 46). The house is L-shaped with a shallow hip roof and large overhanging eaves. It is constructed of brick and mahogany trim. A carport counterbalances the living room wing. Built on the brow of a hill, the house could also be termed a raised Usonian since there is a lower level housing the utilities. Prior to building, the Goddards did their homework by looking at the Anthony house in Benton Harbor; the Palmer house, then under construction; and the Galesburg-Parkwyn houses in order to determine a design and materials that would best serve their needs.

Fig. 45. Donald Schaberg house, Okemos, Michigan, 1952.

In 1955, Frank Lloyd Wright was commissioned by Dorothy Turkel to design a house in the Palmer Woods section of Detroit. After reading Wright's architectural ideology in *The Natural House,* she contacted him. The house was planned for a lot 200 feet wide just falling within the guidelines established by Wright regarding city lots. The design of the Turkel house called for the Usonian Automatic, one of few built, which was completely constructed out of concrete blocks including the ceilings. Wright served to reinforce this technique with a talk he gave in Detroit the year the house was being built: ''Concrete reinforced with fibers of steel is the body of our modern world in any form. Concrete with steel fibers embedded in it, which is very like your own structure or the structure of the tree or any structure nature indulges in, is going to be the body of our modern world.''[13]

Fig. 46. Lewis Goddard house, Plymouth, Michigan, 1952.

An L-shaped, two-story, four-thousand-square-feet structure, the Turkel house (Fig. 47) dovetails nicely with the lot. The interior space is defined by a two-foot-square module. It is perpendicular to the road like the Goetsch-Winckler house in Okemos. An inconspicuous entrance is placed on the west side of the house almost identical to the Meyer May house in Grand Rapids. There are 37 different block designs. The first block took three months to develop and the subsequent 6,000 blocks were fabricated on the site. This house once again, like the Galesburg-Parkwyn group, recalls Wright's concrete block houses in California. "... Hollyhock house [in Los Angeles] was to be a natural house in the changed circumstances and naturally built; native to the region of California as the house in the Middle West had been native to the Middle West."[14] This raises a question, however, as to whether concrete block can be considered a "native" material for the temperate climate of the Midwest. With a high humidity factor, salts leach out of the concrete, combining with the moisture, to form salt crystals on the exterior.

When the 128-foot foundation of the Turkel house was poured, it was within three-sixteenths of an inch of being perfectly level. The most striking feature of the house consists of two walls in the living room broken up into 177 two-foot-square grid-like windows rising to a height of 15 feet. The wall opposite is covered with two-foot squares of Philippine mahogany panels. A balcony in the upstairs hall overlooks the room. The ceilings also conform to the module with recessed panels. When the house was being built, the public response was incredulous awe in the exclusive neighborhood of half-timber, Tudor houses. Dorthy Turkel was unconcerned about the visual incongruity her house provoked in the neighborhood. She was open to new ideas and rejected what was considered more acceptable and fashionable in domestic architecture.

Frank Lloyd Wright's final mark in Michigan was a house he designed in 1957 for Carl Schultz in St. Joseph. Schultz, owner of Benton Harbor Malleable Industries, undoubtedly became familiar with the architecture of Frank Lloyd Wright when he saw the house Wright designed for fellow businessman Howard Anthony in Benton Harbor. Thereupon, Schultz commissioned Wright to design his house on a site overlooking the St.

Balthazar Korab

Fig. 47. Dorothy Turkel house, Detroit, Michigan, 1955.

Joseph River. Wright's plan was typical of the later Usonian Houses designed for clients beyond moderate means: a 20 by 32-foot living room; diningroom; three bedrooms; library; and game room. The projected cost of the house in 1958 was $75,000.00—a considerable amount of money for a domestic dwelling that year. Schultz, however, was thrifty enough to salvage some 50,000 bricks from one of his demolished industrial buildings, and used them in the construction of the house. It is the quintessence of the Prairie House made contemporary (Fig. 48): very low to the ground, with a widely overhanging hip roof; ribbon fenestration; and the massive chimney-utility core further anchoring the house to the site. The most dramatic feature of the house is a cantilevered terrace (Fig. 49), beyond the living room, projecting out over a steep hill that slopes down to the St. Joseph River. ''This building is a late example of the inspiration of a site, the cooperation of an intelligent, appreciative client ...''[14], said Wright about his masterpiece ''Fallingwater.'' This acknowledgement can be equally applicable to the Schultz house—the final exclamation point of Wright's work in Michigan.

Frank Lloyd Wright died April 9, 1959. In the December, 1959 issue of the *AIA Monthly Bulletin, Michigan Society of Architects,* Eugene Masselink, secretary of the Frank Lloyd Wright Foundation wrote from Taliesin in Wisconsin:

> ... Within the last decade particularly, Mr. Wright designed more homes for this neighbor state of ours than for any other one part of the country. The communities he planned for Parkwyn Village in Kalamazoo and the Galesburg homes near Kalamazoo are thriving testimony of the inevitable decentralization Mr. Wright prophesied in his book, *The Living City*.[15]

Frank Lloyd Wright sought in architecture a new truth based on principles that acted in the interest of the human being. His architecture in Michigan, along with intelligent clients open to new esthetic ventures, played an important part in finding that truth. When Wright designed individual houses, he formalized an architecture that reflected and molded the character of the inhabitant. With this unique group of Usonian Houses in Michigan, a vision was realized that became an efflorescence.

Fig. 48. Carl Schultz house, St. Joseph, Michigan, 1957.

Fig. 49. Schultz house, balcony.

1. Edgar Tafel, *Years With Frank Lloyd Wright: Apprentice To Genius,* Dover Publications, N.Y., p. 126.

2. Loren Pope, ''The Love Affair of a Man and His House,'' *House Beautiful,* August, 1948, p. 34.

3. Letter, James Edwards to Frank Lloyd Wright, August 2, 1948, courtesy of the Frank Lloyd Wright Archives.

4. Letter, James Edwards to Frank Lloyd Wright, April 28, 1949, courtesy of the Frank Lloyd Wright Archives.

5. Letter, Howard Anthony to Frank Lloyd Wright, April 19, 1949, courtesy of the Frank Lloyd Wright Archives.

6. Letter, Frank Lloyd Wright, to Howard Anthony, January 18, 1950, courtesy of the Frank Lloyd Wright Archives.

7. Letter, Howard Anthony to Frank Lloyd Wright, September 17, 1949, courtesy of the Frank Lloyd Wright Archives.

8. Letter, Ina Morriss Harper to Frank Lloyd Wright, November 7, 1948, courtesy of the Frank Lloyd Wright Archives.

9. Letter, Ina Morriss Harper to Frank Lloyd Wright, November 16, 1948, courtesy of the Frank Lloyd Wright Archives.

10. Mary Palmer, *The Work of Frank Lloyd Wright,* The Midland Art Association, Midland, Michigan, 1959.

11. Mary Palmer, ''The Wright Choice,'' *The Prairie House Journal,* Domino's Farms, Ann Arbor, Michigan, April, 1987.

12. Frank Lloyd Wright, Address to the Junior Chapter of the American Institute of Architects, New York City, 1952.

13. Frank Lloyd Wright, ''Town Hall Lecture, Ford Auditorium, Detroit, Oct. 21, 1957,'' *AIA Monthly Bulletin, Michigan Society of Architects,* December, 1957, p. 29.

14. Edgar Kaufmann and Sam Raeburn, editors, *Frank Lloyd Wright: Writings and Buildings,* Meridian Books, N.Y., p. 272.

15. Eugene Masselink, *AIA Monthly Bulletin, Michigan Society of Architects,* December, 1959.

□ □ □

Houses designed by Frank Lloyd Wright in Michigan

Arthur Heurtley cottage, Les Cheneaux (Marquette Is.), 1896
George Gerts double cottage, Whitehall, 1902
Walter Gerts cottage, Whitehall, 1902
* Edward C. Waller summer residence (scheme #1), Charlevoix, 1902
* Edward C. Waller summer residence (scheme #2), Charlevoix, 1903
Meyer May house, 450 Madison, S.E., Grand Rapids, 1908
William Burke house (demolished), Three Rivers, 1908, reworking of Frank Lloyd Wright design by Marion Mahony
*Larwell house, Muskegon, 1909
* Edward C. Waller bathing pavilion, Charlevoix, 1909
Joseph Bagley summer residence, Grand Beach, 1916
W.S. Carr summer residence, Grand Beach, 1916
Ernest Vosburgh summer residence, Grand Beach, 1916
* Behn summer house, Grand Beach, 1916
* Converse summer house, Palisades Park, 1916
Abby Beecher Roberts house, "Deertrack," Marquette, 1936
* Usonian development of seven houses for Brauner, Garrison, Goetsch-Winckler, Hause, Newman, Panshin, and Van Dusen, Okemos, 1938
Goetsch-Winckler house, 4331 Hulett Rd., Okemos, 1939
Gregor Affleck house, 1925 North Woodward Ave., Bloomfield Hills, 1941
Carl Wall, "Snowflake" house, 12305, Beck Rd., Plymouth, 1941
* Walter Dayre music studio, Oakland County, 1941
* Cooperative Homesteads, Madison Heights, 1942
* Circle Pines Camp, Cloverdale, 1942
* George Berdan house, Ludington, 1945
* Malcolm Dana, President's House, Olivet College, Olivet, 1946
Erling Brauner house, 2504 Arrowhead Rd., Okemos, 1946
Melvyn Maxwell Smith 5045 Ponvalley Rd., Bloomfield Hills, 1946
* Walter Dayre house and music pavilion (scheme #2), Oakland County, 1946
* Housing for State Teachers College, Lansing, 1946
* J.J. Garrison house, Lansing, 1946
* C.O. Hause house, Lansing, 1946
* Newman house (Usonia I), Lansing, 1946
* Van Dusen house (Usonia I), Lansing, 1946
* Alexis Panshin house, Lansing, 1946
* R.H. Keith house, Oakland County, 1947
* Auto display room and workshop for Roy Wetmore, Detroit, 1947
Amy Alpaugh house, North Peterson Park Rd., Northport, 1947
Galesburg Village master plan, 1947
Parkwyn Village master plan, Kalamazoo, 1947
Erling Brauner house, 2527 Arrowhead Rd., Okemos, 1948
* C.W. Muehlberger house, East Lansing, 1948
* Frederick Margolis house, Kalamazoo, 1948
* Talbot Smith house, Ann Arbor, 1948
Robert Levin house, 2816 Taliesin Dr., Kalamazoo, 1948
Samuel Eppstein house, 11098 Hawthorne Dr., Galesburg, 1948
Eric Pratt house, 11036 Hawthorne Dr., Galesburg, 1948
Howard Anthony house, 1150 Miami Rd., Benton Harbor, 1949
James Edwards house, 2504 Arrowhead Rd., Okemos 1949
Ward McCartney house, 2662 Taliesin Dr., Kalamazoo, 1949
David Weisblat house, 11185 Hawthorne Dr., Galesburg, 1949
* Goetsch-Winckler house (scheme #2), 1949
Eric Brown house, 2806 Taliesin Dr., Kalamazoo, 1950
Ina Morriss Harper house, 207 Sunnybank, St. Joseph, 1950
Curtis Meyer house, 11108 Hawthorne Dr., Galesburg, 1950
William Palmer house, 227 Orchard Hills Dr., Ann Arbor, 1950
Robert Winn house, 2822 Taliesin Dr., Kalamazoo, 1950
* Dale O'Donnell house, East Lansing, 1950
* Brainerd Sabin house, Battle Creek, 1950
* Donald Schaberg house (scheme #1), Okemos, 1950
* Lawrence Strong house, Kalamazoo, 1950
* Louis B. Hall house, Ann Arbor, 1951
* Gregor Affleck house (scheme #2), 1952
* Lawrence Swan house, near Detroit, 1952
Don Schaberg house, 1155 Wrightwind Dr., Okemos, 1952
James Edwards house, 2504 Arrowhead Rd., Okemos, 1952
Lewis Goddard house, 12221 Beck Rd., Plymouth, 1952
* Edgar S. Lee house, Midland, 1953
* George Dlesk house, Manistee, 1953
* Leonard Jankowski house (scheme #1), Oakland County, 1955
* Oscar Miller house, Milford, 1955
Dorothy Turkel house, 2760 W. Seven Mile Rd., Detroit, 1955
Carl Schultz house, 2704 Highland Court, St. Joseph, 1957
* Stanley Hartman house, Lansing, 1957
* Allen Zieger house, Grosse Ile, 1957
* Pat Hanley, airplane hanger, 1957
* Wesley Libbey house, Grand Rapids, 1958

* *Indicates houses that were not built.*

Appendix

Appendix A

Frank Lloyd Wright gave many talks in Michigan promoting his philosophy of architecture and work throughout the state. His candor, honesty, and outspoken character left an indelible mark on his audience. Those who were present still recount the experience today.

April 25, 1935: Cranbrook Academy of Art, Bloomfield Hills.

November 26, 1935: Peoples Church, East Lansing, sponsored by the Art Department, Michigan State College.

April 27, 1937: sponsored by the Art Teachers Club of Grand Rapids.

April 29, 1937: Cranbrook Academy of Art, Bloomfield Hills.

March 22, 1945: Rackham Memorial Building, under the auspices of the Michigan Society of Architects, Detroit.

March 23, 1945: Cranbrook Academy of Art, Bloomfield Hills.

November 2, 1947: Kalamazoo Art Center, under the auspices of the Kalamazoo Art Center in co-sponsorship with the Parkwyn Village and Galesburg Country Homes Associations.

November 4, 1947: Michigan State College, sponsored by the Art Department, East Lansing.

May 24, 1949: Ladies Literary Club auditorium, sponsored by the Friends of American Art, Grand Rapids.

May 14, 1951: Music Hall, Detroit, under the auspices of the Architectural Club, student branch of the A.I.A., Lawrence Institute of Technology.

May 27, 1954: Masonic Temple, sponsored by the Detroit Chapter/AIA. and Grinells, Detroit.

October 21, 1957: Detroit Town Hall series, Ford Auditorium, sponsored by Detroit Chapter/AIA.

October 22, 1957: School of Architecture, University of Michigan, Ann Arbor.

Fig. 50. Frank Lloyd Wright with Eliel Saarinen at Cranbrook, April 25, 1935.

Courtesy of Cranbrook Archives

Frank Lloyd Wright made numerous trips to Cranbrook and a mutual respect developed between Wright and Saarinen. The design of Kingswood School for girls at Cranbrook by Saarinen was inspired by Wright with its low hipped-roof, overhanging eaves and horizontal bands of windows. Saarinen's wife, Loja, also wove the carpeting and fabrics that Wright designed for Edgar Kaufmann's office in Pittsburgh. Wright saw at Cranbrook a potential roster of students who might join his own fellowship.

Appendix B

Mamah Borthwick Cheney, the second woman in Frank Lloyd Wright's life whom he referred to as his kindred spirit, also had an association with Michigan. She attended the University of Michigan receiving her BA in 1892 and MA in 1893. She then went on to teach English, French and history at Port Huron High School in Port Huron, Michigan from 1893 to 1896. She was popular with the high school students and considered good natured. In an issue of *The Tatler,* the high school paper, a story appeared recounting Miss Borthwick's attendance at the Military Street Skating Rink in the winter of 1893. The crowds were watching one night with interest at ''the graceful contortions of a handsome young High School teacher'' ... when she suddenly swayed and fell with a ''wild shriek'' on the ice. The article ended with a quatrain:

''She is a sweet school teacher
with eyes like a gem,
But she is from Chicago
Where the girls have feet like men.''

After leaving Port Huron, Mamah Borthwick was married in 1899 to Edwin Cheney whom she met at the Universtiy of Michigan. They commissioned Frank Lloyd Wright in 1904 to design their house at 520 North East Avenue in Oak Park, Illinois which provided the setting for Mamah's love affair with Wright that lead to their subsequent ''spiritual hegira'' to Europe in 1910. Upon their return to the United States in 1911, they retired to Taliesin in Spring Green, Wisconsin to take up residence. On August 14, 1914, Mamah was visited by her three children, John and Martin by Edwin, and Jessica, an adopted daughter of Mamah's sister Lizzie who died during childbirth. Mamah and the children were all killed on August 14, 1914 by a servant who went beserk at Taliesin. As reported later in an article in the *Chicago Tribune:* ''...She for whom Taliesin had first taken form and her two children—gone.''

□ □ □

Fig. 51. Frank Lloyd Wright with Bob Ziegelman at the University of Michigan, October 22, 1957.

Bob Ziegelman, who was the president of his class at the School of Architecture at the University of Michigan, heard that Wright was going to speak in Detroit on October 21st. He took the initiative and called Taliesin asking Wright if he would come to Ann Arbor and speak to the students. Wright said he would provided there were no teachers present and that it would be in the drafting room. When Ziegelman went to Detroit to pick up Wright, he introduced himself. "Mr. Wright, I'm Bob Ziegelman from the University of Michigan," to which Wright responded, "You have my sympathy." During his talk, Wright said to the students, "There is nothing I can do for you. There is nothing I can do for any school." When asked by one of the students to define beauty, Wright said, "I wouldn't define it. To define it is to confine it."

Index

Affleck, Gregor, 46-47, **48, 49**
Alpaugh, Amy, 53-58, **56, 57**
Anthony, Howard, 76, **77**
Bagley, Joseph, 25, **26**
Borthwick, Mamah, 100
Brauner, Erling, 50, 53, **54**
Brown, Eric, 81, **83**
Burke, William, 14, 21, **24**
Butler, Samuel, 32
Carr, W.S., 25, 27, **28**
Cheney, Mamah, see Borthwick
Coonley, Avery, 14
Cooperative Homesteads, 43-46, **45**
Edwards, James, 73-76, **75**
Emerson, Ralph Waldo, 32
Eppstein, Samuel, 61, **64**
Fallingwater, 12, 47
Ford, Edsel, 23
Ford, Henry, 23-24
Galesburg project, 58-59
Garrison, Ann, 38
Gerts, George, 11, **15**
Gerts, Walter, 12, **16**
Goddard, Lewis, 87, **89**
Goetsch, Alma, 35-39, **37**, 74
Green, Aaron, 43, 46
Harper, Ina M., 76, 78, **79, 80**
Heurtley, Arthur, 11, **13**
Hollyhock House, 90
Holst, Herman von, 25
Jacobs, Herbert, 32, 44, 67, 83
Johnson, Herbert, 32
Kaufmann, Edgar, Sr.,32
Kaufmann, Edgar, Jr., 35
Lautner, John, 33
Levin, Robert, 59-61, **60, 62**
Lutomski, Mary (Affleck), 47
Mahony, Marion, 21, 23, **24**
May, Meyer, 14, 17, **19, 20,** 90
McCartney, Ward, 61, **63**
Meyer, Curtis, 83, **83**
Meyer, Lillian, 58
Midway, Gardens, 17
Okemos project, 35
Palmer, Mary, 83
Palmer, William, 83, 85, **86**
Panshin, Alexis, 39, **40**
Parkwyn Village, 59-61, **60**
Peters, Wesley, 65
Pratt, Eric, 61, 65, **66**
Roberts, Abby Beecher, 33-35, **34**
Roberts, Mary, 33
Robie, Frederick, 14, **19**
Saarinen, Eliel, 53, **99**
Schaberg, Donald, 85, 87, **88**
Schultz, Carl, 90, 92, 93, **94**
Smith, Melvyn M., 65-71, **68, 69**
Thoreau, Henry David, 65
Turkel, Dorothy, 89, 90, **91**
Turner, Harold, 38, 39, 46
Vosburgh, Ernest, 25, **29**
Wall, Carl, 47, 50, **51**
Waller, Edward C. 12, **17, 18**
Weisblat, David, **60,** 61, 65, **67**
Wills, C. Harold, 23, 25
Winckler, Kathrine, 35-39, **37**
Winn, Robert, **82,** 83
Ziegelman, Bob, **101**

Bold page numbers indicate photos or drawings.